Contractual Correspondence for Architects and Project Managers

Fourth Edition

Contractual Correspondence for Architects and Project Managers

Fourth Edition

David Chappell

BA(Hons Arch), MA(Arch), MA(Law), PhD, RIBA
David Chappell Consultancy Limited

Blackwell Publishing

Editorial offices:
Blackwell Publishing Ltd, 9600 Garsington Road, Oxford OX4 2DQ, UK
   Tel: +44 (0)1865 776868
Blackwell Publishing Inc., 350 Main Street, Malden, MA 02148-5020, USA
   Tel: +1 781 388 8250
Blackwell Publishing Asia Pty Ltd, 550 Swanston Street, Carlton, Victoria 3053, Australia
   Tel: +61 (0)3 8359 1011

First edition published 1983 by The Architectural Press Ltd
Second edition published 1989 by Legal Studies & Services Ltd
Third edition published 1996 by Blackwell Science Ltd
Fourth edition published 2006 by Blackwell Publishing Ltd

ISBN-10: 1-4051-3514-X
ISBN-13: 978-1-4051-3514-6

Library of Congress Cataloging-in-Publication Data
Chappell, David.
   Contractual correspondence for architects and project managers / David Chappell. – 4th ed.
      p.   cm.
   Includes index.
   ISBN-13: 978-1-4051-3514-6 (hardback : alk. paper)
   ISBN-10: 1-4051-3514-X (hardback : alk. paper)   1. Architectural contracts–Great Britain–Forms.
2. Architects–Legal status, laws, etc.–Great Britain–Forms.   I. Title.
   KD1641.A65C45 2006
   344.41′0176172–dc22   2005024848

A catalogue record for this title is available from the British Library

Set in 10/13 pt Palatino
by SNP Best-set Typesetter Ltd., Hong Kong
Printed and bound in Great Britain
by TJ International, Padstow, Cornwall

The publisher's policy is to use permanent paper from mills that operate a sustainable forestry policy, and which has been manufactured from pulp processed using acid-free and elementary chlorine-free practices. Furthermore, the publisher ensures that the text paper and cover board used have met acceptable environmental accreditation standards.

For further information on Blackwell Publishing, visit our website:
www.thatconstructionsite.com

Contents

Preface to the Fourth Edition

This was the first book I wrote. The first edition, with all its limitations, was extremely well received, particularly by architects, for whom it was written. It clearly filled a need for a handy book to help solve a few common problems. The somewhat enlarged second and third editions enjoyed continuing success and I sincerely hope that this new version will continue to act as a lifebelt in tricky situations. Many architects have been kind enough to tell me that it has been helpful.

The revisions have again been extensive. There has been much case law in the nine years since the third edition and, although this is not a legal textbook and contains no references to decided cases, they have been taken into account together with the Housing Grants, Construction and Regeneration Act 1996 and other legislation in framing the advice and model letters. In addition, the Joint Contracts Tribunal has issued a completely revised set of standard contracts. The advice and letters have been amended accordingly.

There is always criticism of the idea of model letters and the use of rather formal language in those letters. I remain firmly unrepentant on both issues. I have never advocated the use of model letters without the input of some brain activity. Circumstances and people demand differing approaches. Having said that, there is no doubt that model letters, sensibly used, are a tremendous aid to a busy practitioner. As for the language: wherever possible I have used the wording of the contract. This makes clear to the recipient that the letter is written pursuant to the appropriate clause. In general I have tried to be clear, concise and precise. It is for the user to make whatever amendments may seem fit in the circumstances. Informality in contractual correspondence is rarely, if ever, warranted, but in any case my informality is not yours and it would be out of place in a book like this.

There are many good contractual handbooks available to assist architects to carry out their duties properly. Contractual handbooks and procedural manuals, however, are intended to ensure that jobs proceed smoothly or, at any rate, within the prescribed limits of normal procedures. When things go wrong, the architect must turn to the legal textbooks, which require time and knowledge to study. It need hardly be said that the standard legal textbooks are not written by practitioners of architecture.

Between the two extremes, a smooth contract or a catastrophe, there is a gap which this book attempts to fill. It is based on the fact that architects, contractors, consultants and clients will forget things, do them at the wrong time or simply make mistakes. In addition, numerous problems arise which the architect cannot foresee. Problems tend to follow a pattern. I have personally encountered or observed most of the situations set out on the pages which follow. The intention is to help architects extricate themselves from difficulties in the most practical way.

This is not a legal textbook. The opinions expressed are my own and I make no claim to infallibility. Adjudication, court and arbitration proceedings are fraught with uncertainty. Try not to be a test case. If in doubt you should always take sound advice.

The following points should be borne in mind when using this book:

- For ease of reference, the book follows the RIBA Plan of Work. Items are located where one would normally expect to find them
- JCT Standard Building Contract 'With Quantities 2005 edition (SBC)' is assumed to have been used. All items are applicable to the Without Quantities edition. The chief difference, noted in the text, is that schedules of work or a specification is used instead of bills of quantities
- Notes and alternatives have been given, where necessary, to show how the items are applicable when the JCT 2005 editions of the Intermediate Building Contract (IC), Intermediate Building Contract with Contractor's Design (ICD), Minor Works Building Contract (MW) or Minor Works Building Contract with Contractor's Design (MWD) are used. Where there are differences, additional notes are added under the headings IC, ICD, MW or MWD as appropriate. Thus if the comments under SBC, IC and ICD are the same, but MW and MWD required different comments, only the main text and a reference to MW and MWD would be given
- The 2004 updates of The Standard Form of Agreement for the Appointment of an Architect 1999 (SFA/99) and the Conditions of Engagement 1999 (CE/99) are assumed to have been used and the appropriate scales and terms of engagement agreed with the client
- It is assumed that the contractor is a corporate body and is referred to as 'it' in the text
- Numbers in brackets in headings and text refer to the numbers of the relevant letters
- Every letter should have a heading, clearly stating the job title. Only letter **1** has been shown in this way to avoid needless repetition

No attempt has been made to cover the perfectly routine matters adequately covered by other manuals. See the author's *Standard Letters in Architectural Practice* for more routine matters. The presentation is a series of problems. It is hoped that the inclusion of a large number of standard letters will be helpful, not only for use as model letters to deal with specific difficulties, but in indicating the kind of letter suitable for similar, although not identical, situations. Each letter should be adjusted in tone to suit the recipient. The Appendices contain sections on writing letters and making decisions.

I wish to thank all the people with whom I have ever worked, all the contractors, sub-contractors, suppliers, quantity surveyors, engineers, the people who have read earlier editions of this book and all the thousands of architects who have telephoned me with problems for helping to crystallise the main problems this book should address. Most of all, I thank my wife, Margaret, who bears with me writing books like this.

David Chappell
David Chappell Consultancy Limited
Wakefield
August 2005

Also new to the fourth edition of *Contractual Correspondence for Architects and Project Managers* is a free CD-ROM, inclusive of all the letters found in the text. All letters are compatible for use with Microsoft® Word and Wordperfect® on IBM-PC and Macintosh® machines. Additionally, every letter can be linked to directly from the table of contents list.

A Appraisal

A1 Client's bona fides: in doubt (1)

New clients often make appearances quite suddenly and you may know little or nothing about them. The request for your services may come in the form of a letter, telephone call or personal approach. Beware of the client who has an aversion to writing letters and who will only deal with you by telephone or in person. That kind of client hates to leave a trail of any sort.

Bearing in mind that many problems between architect and client owe their origins to an initial misunderstanding, you must go through the normal procedure of appointment including a very clear agreement on its precise terms and the fees payable (if you are dealing with a private client, see A2). The fact that your client is well known, and even respected, in his or her own profession is no guarantee that you will be paid your fees.

If you are at all uncertain about your client's ability to pay your fees, there are two things you can do immediately after receiving the initial approach:

- Take out references
- Ask the client for a payment on account

Both procedures require careful consideration before putting them into operation. References can usually be obtained through your own bank on a confidential basis but your prospective client may well discover that you have been making enquiries and take offence. There are also firms who specialise in providing this kind of information. Much depends upon the type of client. Nowadays, the taking up of references is commonplace before any sort of credit is extended. You alone will be in a position to gauge your client's probable reaction.

The alternative, which is much favoured by the legal profession, is sometimes a good way to test the serious intentions of a previously unknown client. If you hear nothing further, your suspicions were probably well founded. If your client proceeds with the meeting, you must be sure to have a clear agreement of the sum payable on account written into your terms of appointment. The precise sum will depend upon your assessment of:

- The size of the job
- The client

1
Letter from architect to client, if bona fides in doubt

Dear

<u>Proposed office block at Back Road, Metrotown</u>

Thank you for your letter [*amend as appropriate if the approach was by telephone or in person*] of [*insert date*] instructing me to carry out architectural services in connection with the above project.

I should be pleased to visit you/see you at this office [*delete as appropriate*] to discuss your detailed requirements and my terms of appointment. I ask for a payment on account of [*insert percentage*] of the estimated total fees[1] at the time of signing the agreement.

A copy of the RIBA Standard Form of Agreement for the Appointment of an Architect[2] is enclosed. When you have had the opportunity to peruse it, perhaps you will telephone me to arrange a convenient date and time for our meeting.

Yours faithfully

[[1] *You may prefer to insert an actual sum of money – it can avoid disputes.*
[2] *Insert whether SFA/99, CE/99 or SW/99 and 2004 update.*]

Finally, you must be sure to get your payment before starting work or writing the letter will be a waste of time.

A2   If your client is a private individual (a consumer) (2)

If your client is acting in a personal capacity when engaging you, in other words, if your client is a consumer, rather than a firm, partnership or company, you should be aware that your contract is subject to the Unfair Terms in Consumer Contracts Regulations 1999. Under the Regulations, a term which is not individually negotiated with your client will be regarded as unfair if it causes significant imbalance in the parties' rights to the consumer's detriment. An unfair term will not be binding on your client.

The difficulty is that a term which has been drafted in advance, for example in SW/99, will always be considered as not being individually negotiated. Therefore, it is essential that you sit down with your client and carefully explain every single term in your appointment document. You must confirm in writing to your client that you have carried out this exercise and that the client has agreed the terms or amendments to them. Particular terms could be singled out for attention; for example, adjudication, any terms restricting the client's right to set-off against payments, and any terms which purport to restrict your liability. However, the safest way is to individually agree every term. If you can get the client to confirm that all terms are negotiated, so much the better, but in practice many client are averse to writing letters.

Very often, the client may be a person of intelligence with a responsible job. Your client may be experienced in business or even a solicitor or a barrister. It makes no difference to the principle. Such a person is regarded in law as a consumer. It seems to be ignoring the facts to take that view; an experienced and sophisticated businessman or woman is, in reality, quite capable of reading a contract and deciding whether legal advice is required. However, if the matter came before the courts, there would be no point in putting forward that argument.

A3   Fee recovery (3), (4), (5), (6), (Fig. 1)

A difficult problem, which should be considered at the beginning of every project, is how to collect fees. Theoretically, you will submit invoices for amounts and at intervals previously agreed (hopefully under an RIBA standard form) and your client will pay. It seldom happens quite like that. Fees more often have to be coaxed or threatened from your client depending on circumstances. It is assumed that you have entered into a proper fee agreement before starting work. If not, you are not so much asking for trouble as laying a red carpet and begging it to come through your door.

The manner and timing of payments should be part of your agreement. Your client may well appreciate being able to make regular payments because it

2
Letter from architect to client, confirming that terms have been negotiated

Dear

[*insert appropriate heading*]

I refer to our meeting yesterday and confirm that I took the opportunity to go through the RIBA Appointment document SFA/99/ CE/99/ SW/99 [*delete as applicable*], 2004 update, with you in detail and that I explained each clause and its significance to you. You were satisfied that you understood the whole of the document.

[*Add either:*]

I further confirm that you did not require any amendments to the terms.

[*Or:*]

I further confirm that we agreed that certain terms should be amended.

[*Then:*]

A copy of the final version of the Appointment is enclosed for you to check, sign and date where indicated and return to me.

Yours faithfully

enables the programming of the client's financial commitment more accurately. Once you have agreed upon a system of regular payments, send accounts regularly and insist on payment. It makes sense to send out all your accounts on a monthly basis. One advantage of a regular fee commitment is that you will have early warning if your client misses a payment. Remember that if your client does not pay you, that is a breach of contract. A sign that your client may be in financial difficulties is sudden questioning of your fee accounts without good reason. Learn to recognise the signs and act accordingly.

You should set up your own system of collecting fees. As a guide, you could use the following procedure, but be ready to vary it depending upon your personal knowledge of your client:

- Send out fee accounts as soon as you can and keep a chart of all fees billed and outstanding with notes of reminders **(Fig. 1)**
- Send a first reminder letter one month after the date of the fee account **(3)**
- Send a second reminder seven days later **(4)**
- After a further seven days, telephone or visit your client if the amount warrants it. At this time state that you must have your fee within seven days
- Seven days later send a letter threatening legal action **(5)**
- Seven days later take legal or other action

If you have reason to believe that you will not be paid, you should curtail the reminders and threaten legal or other action at an early date. Clearly, if you do take action through the courts, by arbitration or adjudication to obtain payment, it is extremely unlikely that your client will commission you again. Splendid; if you have any sense, you will not accept such a commission even if offered. Always remember that your survival is at stake so act promptly.

If your client tells you, after the first reminder, that there is a temporary financial embarrassment, but is confident of paying you within, say, a month or six weeks or in instalments, you will have to use your judgment whether to accept the offer. If you do, get it in writing. If there is a failure to pay as promised, take immediate action. On no account agree to postpone your fees in this way twice with the same client and do not consider giving extra time to pay if you are not told of the difficulties until you threaten action.

This is merely a guide. How you react in any given set of circumstances is for you to decide. Remember that many individuals and firms make a habit of paying at the last possible moment. It makes good economic sense to them and they can be very plausible in formulating excuses.

In most cases you will recover fees after you have sent one or two reminders and certainly before you put your threat of legal action into effect. There will always be some instances, however, where legal action is your only hope. Every architect should have a detailed knowledge of the Housing Grants, Construction and Regeneration Act 1996, which applies to architectural services and requires every contract to have calculable dates when payment is due and the final date for payment. It does not apply to residential contracts, but the RIBA

Client	Fees billed	Date	First reminder (4 weeks)	Date	Second reminder (7 days)	Date	Threaten legal action (7 days)	Date	Take action (7 days)	Date
A Ltd	25,000	30.05.05	Yes	27.06.05	Yes	04.07.05	Yes	11.07.05	Adjudication, arbitration or litigation as appropriate	18.07.05
B LLP	10,700	30.05.05	Yes	27.06.05	PAID	29.06.05				
Ms C	3,000	30.05.05	Yes	27.06.05	PAID	01.07.05				
D Ltd	4,500	30.05.05	PAID	20.06.05						
Mr E	7,200	30.05.05	PAID	24.06.05						
Mrs F	300	30.05.05	PAID	02.06.05						
G Ltd	9,000	30.05.05	Yes	27.06.05	↑		Yes	04.07.05	PAID	06.07.05
H Ltd	6,400	30.05.05	Yes	27.06.05	Yes	04.07.05	PAID	06.07.05		
J Partners	2,800	30.05.05	Yes	27.06.05	Yes	04.07.05	PAID	08.07.05		
K Ltd	12,000	06.06.05	PAID	14.06.05						
Miss L	2,500	06.06.05	Yes	27.06.05	PAID	29.06.05				

Fig. 1 Fee recovery chart.

3
Letter from architect to client – first reminder

Dear

[*insert appropriate heading*]

I refer to my fee account dated [*insert date*] in the sum of £ [*insert amount*] which is still outstanding.

You will appreciate that I rely upon clients to settle accounts promptly so that current economic fee rates can be maintained. No doubt the matter has escaped your attention, but I should be pleased if you would let me have your cheque by return of post.

Yours faithfully

4
Letter from architect to client – second reminder

Dear

[*insert appropriate heading*]

I refer to my fee account dated [*insert date*] in the sum of [*insert amount*] and my letter of [*insert date*]. I regret to note that I have not yet received payment.

Would you please give this matter your immediate attention?

Yours faithfully

5
Letter from architect to client – threatening legal action

Dear

[*insert appropriate heading*]

I refer to my fee account dated [*insert date*] in the sum of [*insert amount*] which has not yet been paid despite reminders dated [*insert dates*].

In view of the relationship which exists between us, I have not pursued this matter with the vigour it deserves. Although I have no wish to cause difficulties for you, I must have regard to my own financial position. I regret, therefore, that if I do not receive your cheque for the full amount outstanding by first post on [*insert date seven days following date of letter*], I shall have no alternative but to take whatever steps are necessary to recover the debt including interest and all my costs. I do hope that it will not become necessary.

Yours faithfully

appointment complies with the Act in any event. The provisions in the Act and complying contracts can make fee recovery relatively easy. In addition, architects would be wise to have some knowledge of the Late Payment of Commercial Debts (Interest) Act 1999 which, in the absence of any contractual term giving a substantial remedy, currently permits interest to be charged at 8% above Bank of England Base Rate as existing at the end of June and December each year. In addition a modest lump sum can be recovered in compensation.

If the sum outstanding is substantial, it is a good idea to speak to your legal advisor before you threaten legal action. You may be advised to incorporate a rehearsal of the facts in your letter together with dates of all letters of reminder in order to form a sound base for proceedings whatever the forum. It is often a good idea for your advisor to draft the initial letter for you to send.

Your client may offer to pay a lesser sum than you demand 'in full settlement' of your fee; otherwise, you may be told that you will get nothing. Do not hesitate to accept provided that:

- Your client has accepted that you are owed the full amount *and*
- There is no consideration attached to the payment of the lesser sum

Having received the lesser sum, you can if you so wish take action to recover the remainder. Your letter of acceptance should follow the lines of Letter (6). If, however, you agree to accept a lesser sum 'in full settlement' of fees which the client is disputing, your acceptance is binding because you are both compromising the dispute and consideration is present. The handling of the matter requires great care and a consultation with your legal advisor is indicated.

Of course, it is always better to accept a lesser sum or payment of very small sums stretching to infinity than to waste time and money chasing an insolvent client.

A4   If two separate individuals or companies wish to commission you jointly (7)

This situation arises more frequently than may be thought. Where private persons are concerned, it may involve conversion work required to a building such as a barn or disused church to turn it into two dwellings. Two companies may have the chance to buy a building which is too large for each, but perfect in size to share after refurbishment.

In each case, both parties will have a keen interest in the outcome and both will want to be in a position to give you instructions. Although it is perfectly understandable to take that position, proceeding on that basis is a recipe for disaster. The old adage that no person can serve two masters is perfectly sound. Ideally, the parties should have an agreement prepared for them which states which one will act as client, speaking for both, and subsequently as employer under the building contract. Your agreement should be with that party alone.

6
Letter from architect to client, 'accepting' lesser payment in full satisfaction

Dear

[*insert appropriate heading*]

Thank you for your letter of [*insert date*].

I note that you agree that you owe [*insert amount*]. You have offered me the sum of [*insert amount*] in full satisfaction of my outstanding fees.

I appear to have little alternative but to accept and I look forward to receiving your payment.

Yours faithfully

7
Letter to clients, if two clients wish to commission you jointly

Dear

[*insert appropriate heading*]

Thank you for your letter/I refer to our meeting [*delete as appropriate*] of the [*insert date*].

I have been giving very serious thought to your requirements and the only immediate problem is one of instruction. In other words, there must be one of you who is authorised by the other to give instructions to me and subsequently to act as employer under the building contract. It is probably best if you enter into a joint agreement for that purpose and your solicitors will be able to advise you. You will probably find the exercise of deciding on heads of terms very beneficial, not only in connection with the building, but also the future operation and maintenance.

Obviously, if two separate buildings were involved, you would each commission me and instruct separately. However, where two parties have interests in one building it is not practicable for both to instruct. There may be occasions when the instructions are in conflict. It would not be for me to cast the deciding vote.

Yours faithfully

A5 Appointment, if architect asked to tender on fees (8)

It is now quite common to be asked to provide a lump sum fee quotation before being commissioned to carry out work. This can occur even if you are the sole architect being considered, but it may indicate that several architects are being asked to tender on fees. There is nothing basically wrong with this; it is covered by principle 2 of the RIBA Code of Professional Conduct 2005, Expanded Guidance Note 4.9. The crucial points to observe are:

- Do not quote a fee unless your prospective client has invited you to do so
- Before quoting, you must have enough information to know the kind of work required, its scope and the precise services your client wants you to provide
- You must not fall into the trap of revising your quotation (always downwards of course) to undercut another architect who is quoting for the same service

Some architects still refuse to tender on fees as a matter of principle. Although there is no real evidence that such architects fare any the worse as a result, it is a fact of modern architectural life that most organisations now operate some kind of fee tendering arrangement. Of course, just because you tender on fees to get a job does not mean that you must cut your fees to the bone. Indeed there is every reason why you should not do that. If your quotation is so low that you are unable to provide the level of service which your client expects, you will simply lose money on the project as you fight an impossible battle between time and costs.

An essential preliminary to fee tendering is cost recording. Only by keeping careful records of what it costs you to carry out a job can you hope to produce reasonably accurate forecasts of future work. Detailed staff time sheets are not only a vital component in costing, they also form essential evidence of work done if you are attempting to recover fees on a time basis for additional work. It is not sufficient simply to put 'XYZ Office Block' and a period of 7½ hours against it. You must break the time and tasks down as far as possible. For example: 'Researching floor finish for factory floor – 5 hours; detail of floor/wall junction – 2½ hours'. Until you have this vital information, steer clear of fee tendering or include a generous amount for contingencies.

A6 Brief: difficulty in obtaining decisions (9), (10), (11)

Despite your best efforts, you may find that your client is very slow in giving you decisions or may try to leave decisions to you which only they can make. The situation is probably commonest when dealing with a client who is actually a board of directors, even though they may have agreed that one of their number is to liaise with you.

This situation can arise at any time during the work, but you should identify the signs at the earliest possible moment – i.e. as soon as a decision is late – and take immediate action by writing to your client **(9)**.

8
Letter from architect to client, if asked to tender on fees

Dear

[*insert appropriate heading*]

Thank you for your letter of [*insert date*].

I am pleased to hear that you are considering appointing me as architect for the above project. I am bound by the RIBA Code of Professional Conduct. I must satisfy certain criteria before quoting a fee. In particular, the precise nature and scope of the work must be known together with the services required. Presumably these will pose no problems in this instance.

Naturally, you are most welcome to visit me to discuss the work or, alternatively, you might find it more convenient to meet me at the proposed site. I can supply you with details of some of the jobs undertaken by this office so that you can visit and see the kind of work done. May I suggest that you telephone me to arrange a meeting.

A copy of Standard Form of Agreement for the Appointment of an Architect, 2004 update, is enclosed so that you can form an idea of the services you require.

Yours faithfully

9
Letter from architect to client, if decisions late

Dear

[*insert appropriate heading*]

I refer to my letter/telephone call [*omit as appropriate*] of [*insert date*] requesting [*briefly indicate the decision required*].

It would be appreciated if you would review your arrangements for providing urgent decisions in the interests of avoiding delays and extra costs.

I am sure you will appreciate that, although I am always ready to give you the benefit of my professional advice, there are certain points which must be referred to you.

Yours faithfully

There are a number of important points you should have noted in the letter:

- The date you requested instructions
- The fact that you are still waiting
- Possible delays and additional costs
- Your willingness to give professional advice
- The fact that there are certain decisions you cannot make

If your client is one person, he or she will almost certainly grasp the points immediately and ought to send you the decision by return. Difficulties sometimes continue if your client is a body of people – a large company, local authority, government department, etc. Much depends upon the calibre of your liaison.

If, in spite of your letter, the client replies in some such manner as: 'I leave it to you to use your professional judgment in the matter', beware; what this really means is: 'I cannot make up my mind and I would like you to do it for me and take the blame if the decision is wrong'.

You are being invited to make the decision yourself. It is very tempting to do just that if the matter is urgent and money is being lost. You must resist the temptation because you are getting no indemnity if the decision is wrong – quite the reverse. You are being told that you are expected to take responsibility for a decision (which should be your client's) as part of your normal professional duties. The precise terms of your reply will vary depending upon the nature of the decision and your knowledge of the client. Letter **10** is intended as an example.

If your client continues to evade the question, you must visit and discuss the matter thoroughly. Persist in requiring an immediate decision and, on your return to the office, confirm the instructions back in polite but clear terms.

Failure to obtain decisions or instructions strikes at the very heart of your services, because you are only empowered to act in accordance with your client's requirements. You have no power to make those decisions yourself. Therefore, a failure to obtain decisions is fatal to you continuing to act for your client. If, despite all your best efforts, you cannot obtain instructions or decisions, it is best to give your client an ultimatum before terminating your engagement under the notice provisions in the appointment document **(11)**.

A7   Consultants: client requiring them to be appointed through the architect (12), (13), (14), (15)

Where the work is such that consultants are required, you will advise your client accordingly. From a contractual point of view, the client should appoint consultants directly. However, your client may understandably wish to deal with only one professional to avoid confusion. You may be asked to deal with every aspect of the project yourself, including the appointment of consultants. You must try to persuade your client to appoint directly and set the matter on record **(12)**.

10
Letter from architect to client, if client is reluctant to make a decision

Dear

[*insert appropriate heading*]

Thank you for your letter of [*insert date*].

Naturally, I will give you every professional assistance I can, but there are certain decisions which are, effectively, your instructions to me. Obviously I cannot instruct myself, and, without instructions, I am unable to carry out my professional duty.

In previous letters I have set out the considerations which you should take into account, and there may be others of which you alone are aware. If it will be of assistance, the instruction required can be put simply as follows:

[*Put the decision required as briefly and succinctly as possible in the form of a clear question which can be answered by a straightforward 'yes' or 'no'.*]

I look forward to hearing from you as soon as possible. A delay is now occurring which it could be difficult to make up and will increase the ultimate cost of the project.

Yours faithfully

11
Letter from architect to client, giving ultimatum about decisions

Dear

[*insert appropriate heading*]

I refer to my letters of the [*insert dates*] and my telephone calls of the [*insert dates*] in which I asked you for various decisions. I have explained that these are decisions which only you can make. Without these decisions, effectively I cannot proceed with my services.

Regretfully, if I do not receive the following decisions by 5.00 pm on [*insert date, allowing about two full working days*] I shall be obliged to serve notice of determination of my appointment in accordance with our agreement:

[*insert list of the decisions which you have previously requested, giving brief description to each such as: 'Increase size of boardroom to take fifteen people?'*]

Yours faithfully

12
Letter from architect to client, regarding direct appointment of consultants where RIBA appointment is not used

Dear

[*insert appropriate heading*]

I refer to our recent conversation regarding the necessity to appoint consultants for [*list services*]. I understand that you wish me to appoint consultants for this project through my office.

Such a course of action would be against my advice. I will, in any case, co-ordinate all consultancy services. Fees for other consultants are the same whether appointed directly or through my office.

I strongly advise you to appoint the consultants directly yourself. It is usual practice in construction projects. I am prepared to carry out preliminary negotiations with each consultant and advise you regarding appointment. By so doing, you have direct access to the other professionals for advice should you so wish and, of course, direct recourse to them for any problems which may arise.

Please give this matter further thought and I look forward to hearing from you within the next few days.

Yours faithfully

If you are using one of the RIBA appointment documents, your client, within the appointment, will have agreed to appoint all consultants directly **(13)**.

If the client is adamant that you should provide consultants' services through your office and you agree, you must make sure that:

- You appoint consultants as your client's agent with his agreement **(14)**
- The consultants' contract with you reflects the terms of your contract with your client
- Your client agrees to pay the appropriate additional fees to cover consultants' services
- You obtain an indemnity from the consultant and check that proper insurance cover is in place to back up any claims made against the consultant **(15)**
- Your own professional indemnity insurers are aware of the arrangements

Do not place unlimited faith in clause 3.11 of the conditions in the Standard Form of Agreement for the Appointment of an Architect and expect that the client will always seek redress from the consultant direct for any problem. You are always the most likely first candidate for your client's displeasure in whatever form it may come. Even if the consultant is clearly liable, if your client takes legal action against you, you will be faced with defending it and all the costs and trauma of joining into the proceedings the consultant in question. The difficulty is, of course, that if for some reason your client cannot recover damages from the consultant, you may be faced with the liability yourself.

Other than the first, the above criteria apply with even more force if you offer your client an 'all in' service by engaging consultants as and when you require them. You must always ensure that your client is aware if you intend to delegate work in this way and that your professional indemnity insurers also know and agree to your course of action.

A8   Other architects, if previously commissioned (16), (17)

When asked to take a commission, there is always the possibility that another architect may have been engaged by the client upon the same work. Principles 2 and 3 of the RIBA Code of Professional Conduct cover the position, and Expanded Guidance Notes 4.9 and 7.5 provide some excellent advice.

There are two stages:

- Discover if another architect has been engaged previously and, if so, write to the client **(16)**
- Write to the other architect **(17)**

A matter of particular importance concerns the right to use any information provided by the previous architect. Usually, if the former architect has been paid a sufficient fee, there will be an implied licence for the client to use material,

13
Letter from architect to client, regarding direct appointment of consultants where RIBA appointment is used

Dear

[*insert appropriate heading*]

I refer to our recent conversation regarding the necessity to appoint consultants for [*list services*]. I understand that you wish me to appoint consultants for this project through my office.

Clauses 3.8 and 3.11 of the conditions of the Standard Form of Agreement for the Appointment of an Architect[1] set out the relevant points. You will note that all consultants are to be appointed directly by you which accords with the normal practice. I will carry out preliminary negotiations with each consultant and advise you regarding appointment. Consultancy fees would be the same whether appointed directly or through my office. I will, in any case, co-ordinate all consultancy services.

You have direct access to the other professionals for advice should you so wish and, of course, direct recourse to them for any problems which may arise.

Yours faithfully

[[1] *Where CE/99 is used, insert* Conditions of Engagement for the Appointment of an Architect. *The clause numbers are the same. Where SW/99 is used, insert* Conditions of Appointment for Small Works *and substitute clause numbers '16' for '3.8' and '17' for '3.11'.*]

14
Letter from architect to client, if architect is asked to appoint consultants

Dear

[*insert appropriate heading*]

Thank you for your letter of [*insert date*] in which you instruct me to engage the services of consultants on your behalf. I shall be happy to act as agent for you in this matter. The appointments are now in hand and I shall let you know when the documentation is prepared and ready for signature so that we can discuss it in detail.

[*If an RIBA appointment is used add:*]

May I take this opportunity of drawing your attention to clause 3.11 of the conditions of the RIBA Standard Form of Agreement for the Appointment of an Architect[1], a copy of which is in your possession, which provides that you will hold each consultant responsible for the competence and performance of the services and visits to site.

Yours faithfully

[[1] *Where CE/99 is used, insert* Conditions of Engagement for the Appointment of an Architect. *The clause number is the same. Where SW/99 is used, insert* Conditions of Appointment for Small Works *and substitute clause number '17' for '3.11'.*]

15
Letter from architect to consultant, seeking indemnity

Dear

[*insert appropriate heading*]

I refer to recent discussions regarding your employment as consultant for [*name services*] on the above project.

Before a formal contract of engagement can be drawn up, I require you to provide me with proof that you carry and will continue to carry suitable and adequate professional indemnity insurance in a sum of no less than £ [*insert amount*] for each and every claim. Please signify your willingness to indemnify me against any claims which may be made in respect of the competence and performance of work entrusted to you including visits to site.

Yours faithfully

16
Letter from architect to client, regarding other architects

Dear

[insert appropriate heading]

I am obliged to make reasonable enquiries to discover if you have previously engaged any other architect upon the above work. If so, please let me have written confirmation whether you hold a licence to use any or all of that architect's material (such as drawings, specifications or calculations). Also whether such licence allows me to make use of and, if appropriate, change such material.

If you cannot produce evidence of such a licence, there are three possible ways forward:

1. You obtain such a licence from the former architect; or
2. I proceed without making use of any of the material prepared by the former architect. *[add, if appropriate:]* That will involve making new submissions for statutory permissions; or
3. You provide me with a written indemnity, to the satisfaction of my legal advisor, in respect of any claims of whatsoever nature made in connection with any material prepared by the former architect.

In addition, I need to know if there are any ongoing issues with which the former architect was involved so that I can consider the position.

Perhaps you will confirm the name and address of the former architect so that I may send the necessary notification of my involvement.

Yours faithfully

17
Letter from architect to other architects, regarding former engagement

Dear

[*insert appropriate heading*]

I have been approached/instructed [*omit as appropriate*] by [*insert name of client*] to undertake the above work.

I understand that you were engaged upon this project at one time and this notice is served to comply with any duty I may have under the RIBA Code of Professional Conduct.

Any comments you wish to make in this connection will receive my careful consideration.

Yours faithfully

although it must be borne in mind that the original architect will always retain copyright on what has been prepared. The mere fact that you have been engaged in place of the former architect suggests that there may be no implied licence and the client may be obliged to pay a special licence fee. Few clients will be aware of these considerations and, therefore, they must be informed to protect your own position. You too would be in breach of copyright if you used the former architect's material and there was no licence.

It is also necessary for you to ensure that there are no other outstanding matters for which you might become liable or which might prevent you from accepting the appointment. You must ask your client the direct question. If your client cannot provide the answers your require, you must direct questions to the former architect. In any event, it is courteous and wise to enquire of the former architect whether there are any obstacles to your acceptance of the appointment.

The other architect may simply acknowledge, ignore or state formally that there are no objections. Alternatively, the architect may say, for example, that he or she was never paid. Besides being a useful indication of your own chances of obtaining fees, it is good practice to request your client to discharge previous fees before you take instructions. You have no duty to do this and, if previous fees are the subject of court proceedings or simply in dispute, you would be advised to stand back and make no comments of any kind.

In such a case, however, you would be wise to consider whether you wish to proceed until the previous case is settled. It is not your place, indeed it would be inappropriate for you, to pass moral or other judgments on disputes with which you are not involved, but previous failure to pay may not auger well for your own relations with the client. If you do proceed, a payment on account (as in A1) would appear to be advisable.

A9   Site boundaries: unclear (18), (19)

It is not at all unusual to find that one or more of your client's site boundaries is not clearly defined either on site or on the deeds. It is not part of your normal duty to settle such matters.

If full information is not provided, you may be tempted to carry out your survey anyway using your common sense to fix the boundaries. Resist the temptation. The client must provide you with all necessary information. If it becomes necessary to negotiate with adjoining owners to fix the boundaries, this is best done by the client's solicitor. If you are asked to take part in the negotiations, you are entitled to request an additional fee for your services and you should make the position clear to your client before you accept the request.

A10   Existing property, if urgent repair work required (20)

During your survey of existing property, it may become clear that certain works must be carried out urgently if the integrity of the fabric is to be preserved. As

18
Letter from architect to client, if site boundary not clear

Dear

[*insert appropriate heading*]

I have conducted a general inspection of the above site today. There are parts of the boundary which are not clearly defined. I have looked at the deeds and unfortunately they shed no light on the matter.

Before I carry out a detailed survey, it is essential that the limits of your ownership are properly defined.

A large scale ordnance survey plan of the area is enclosed, noting the principal features – walls, roads, adjacent buildings etc. Perhaps you would be good enough to ask your solicitor to indicate the precise extent of your ownership by drawing a red line around the site and returning the sketch to me as soon as possible. Please show dimensions if available.

Yours faithfully

19
Letter from architect to client, if requested to help in boundary negotiations

Dear

[*insert appropriate heading*]

Thank you for your letter of [*insert date*].

I will be happy to assist in the negotiations with adjoining owners in order to fix the site boundaries. Your own solicitor should take charge of the negotiations and I will be present to advise at any meeting between all parties.

An additional fee at the rate of [*insert amount*] per hour is chargeable for such additional services, and I should be pleased to have your agreement. Clause 5.6 of the conditions of the RIBA Standard Form of Agreement for the Appointment of an Architect[1] refers.

Perhaps you will ask your solicitor to telephone me directly to arrange a meeting.

Yours faithfully

[[1] *Where CE/99 is used, insert* Conditions of Engagement for the Appointment of an Architect. *The clause numbers are the same. Where SW/99 is used, insert* Conditions of Appointment for Small Works *and substitute clause number '22' for '5.6'.*]

20
Letter from architect to client, if urgent repairs required

Dear

[*insert appropriate heading*]

I refer to our telephone conversation of [*insert date*].

During our survey of the above property, it was discovered that [*insert description of the problem as clearly as possible*].

In order to avoid the possibility of collapse [*or insert the appropriate danger*] I strongly advise that immediate work is necessary. In view of the nature and urgency of the work, it is impossible to obtain competitive quotations although the quantity surveyor may be able to give you an indication of the likely cost. I request your agreement to the employment of [*insert name of a suitable contractor or specialist firm*] to carry out the necessary work on site.

If you give me authority on your behalf to employ the above firm, or some other firm which you may care to nominate, I will instruct them to carry out the necessary work and request them to submit accounts directly to you for payment.

Yours faithfully

Copy: Quantity surveyor

soon as this becomes apparent, you should waste no time in informing your client and obtaining instructions. Telephone first and follow up with a letter.

Your client will be unhappy about the prospect of effectively signing a blank cheque, and it may well be possible for you, with the assistance of the quantity surveyor and the firm in question, to obtain some indication of the likely cost. Much depends upon the urgency of the situation, and your letter should be amended accordingly.

A11   Client: if wanting to proceed with inadequate planning permission (21)

It is startling how often a client will try to persuade an architect to proceed with a commission without proper planning permission. It may be that the client has obtained permission in the past and it has lapsed, or permission may have been obtained for a building and the client wants something rather different on the site. Sometimes the client has outline planning permission but is reluctant to seek full planning permission because there are elements of the scheme which might cause problems. There is usually a good reason for the reluctance. This type of client just does not, or will not, see that to proceed under those circumstances is simply asking for trouble, not least because those involved are in breach of planning law. There could also be enormous financial repercussions.

If your client asks you to become involved, you must refuse unless you can include applying for planning permission as part of your brief.

21
Letter from architect to client, if asked to deal with a building for which existing planning permission is inadequate

Dear

[*insert appropriate heading*]

Further to our meeting on the [*insert date*] when you briefed me on your requirements, I said that I was extremely concerned about [*describe the particular problem*]. I have advised you that a failure to comply with planning requirements may result in the enforcement process resulting in demolition of a completed building and/or heavy continuing fines.

Clearly, as a professional person, I cannot be involved in any project if it appears that a deliberate contravention of the planning laws is likely. Be assured that I am ready to assist you in this project if you are content for me to make application to the planning authorities on your behalf.

Please consider the contents of this letter carefully and then telephone me with your decision.

Yours faithfully

B   Strategic Briefing

B1   Brief: unacceptable requirements (22)

A considerable degree of tact is required to obtain a proper brief from your client. At this stage it must be neither too detailed nor too general. Nevertheless, it must be precise, because in the agreement with your client, you undertake to satisfy the brief with your design. Therefore, it is important to know exactly when the brief has been satisfied. Subsequent changes in the brief, as opposed to additional detail, rank as extra work for which additional fees are due.

It is not unusual for a client involved in building for the first time to attempt to impose requirements which are basically whims. The ideas may become so fixed, however, that no design will be considered unless they are incorporated. A parish priest may have a longing for Gothic arches in the new church, a managing director may require a symmetrical elevation to the new office block, the private housebuilder may insist on dormers on the roof. Such requirements are usually completely irrelevant and show a lack of understanding of the architect's true function. You can, of course, resign your commission but that is a drastic step, hardly justified. If you produce a good design, the client will usually realise the initial mistake and be happy to forget that particular obsession as the excellent way in which you have interpreted the requirements becomes apparent. In the meantime, send a tactful letter.

22
Letter from architect to client who has unacceptable requirements

Dear

[*insert appropriate heading*]

I refer to our discussion of [*insert date*] during which your general requirements were noted.

I am proceeding with the feasibility study and strategic brief. If it proves acceptable to you, I will prepare outline proposals for your consideration.

I realise that you are anxious to include [*insert the disputed feature*] and I suggest that, while bearing that in mind, we allow the design to take shape in a purely logical way at first and review the situation at outline proposal stage, when we will have a better understanding of the way the building is developing.

Yours faithfully

C   Outline Proposals

C1   Objections: by client (23)

Undoubtedly, the best way to submit outline proposals is to take them personally to your client and explain them thoroughly. Your client will normally wish to study the proposals and possibly discuss them with colleagues. In due course you can expect to receive comments and sometimes objections to some aspects of your scheme.

If you have done your job properly, the comments should be constructive and the objections minor. If the points are all reasonable, you should have little difficulty in revising your proposals to satisfy them. A problem arises if you consider any objection on the part of the client to be unreasonable. You should revise your scheme as required except for the unreasonable objection and marshal your arguments in the most convincing way.

When faced with your proposals, revised to suit the comments except in one particular, you should have little difficulty in persuading your client of the soundness of your own thinking – provided you have done your homework. Resist any attempt to discuss the problem on the telephone. A face-to-face discussion over the drawings is much more likely to yield fruitful results.

C2   Objections: by planning authority, civic society etc. (24), (25), (26)

At this stage in the project a number of bodies may register objections. The local planning authority is the most obvious, and, in order to achieve the scheme you want, you may be engaged in a considerable amount of discussion. They have their own criteria when confronted with proposals, and some of their concerns may not be yours. Generally, however, they are very helpful in trying to reach a solution.

Avoid a head-on confrontation: it only leads to entrenched positions and eventual refusal. See what can be agreed so as gradually to isolate the main problems. A little patience and diplomacy coupled with a professed understanding of the authority's problems will often succeed in reducing the objection itself to a mere detail. The objections of the planning authority can sometimes be used, if all else fails, to convince the client to see the solution your way. After agreement, always

23
Letter from architect to client, if objection unreasonable

Dear

[*insert appropriate heading*]

Thank you for your useful comments on the outline proposals for the above project.

Most of your suggestions have posed no problems and they have been incorporated in revised proposals.

Only one point has proved difficult to reconcile with the brief as a whole: [*outline the point in question*].

I suggest that the best way to solve the problem is for me to visit you for a thorough discussion. I will telephone you within the next day or so to arrange a suitable time and date.

Yours faithfully

send a revised set of drawings (as many copies as individual authorities require) in confirmation **(24)**.

Civic societies, amenity and environmental groups and the like are a much more subtle problem. Some architects believe that the best policy is to ignore them, but that can be a grave error. They wield great influence, and if you receive an objection from them, the best policy is often to offer to visit the group with plans and models (if possible) and explain the project. It is really a public relations exercise which should not be missed. Once you have shown your interest in their particular concerns, their objections often melt away. Get your client's approval first.

It is easiest to discuss the arrangements with your client and the amenity group by telephone and then confirm by letter. The letters will obviously vary slightly but **25** and **26** can be considered guides.

After the meeting, confirm the results to your client and, if the objections have been withdrawn, to the society to avoid future dispute.

24
Letter from architect to planning authority, after objections

Dear

[*insert appropriate heading*]

I refer to discussions in your department held with [*insert names of the appropriate planning officers*] on [*insert date/s*].

In accordance with the agreement reached at the above meeting(s), I have revised the proposals and enclose [*insert number of drawings they require*] sets of drawings numbers [*insert numbers*]. I understand that you will insert them in place of the original drawings numbers [*insert numbers*] for the consideration of your committee.

Thank you for your co-operation in this matter and I look forward to your approval on [*insert date on which they have agreed to confirm their decision*].

If there are any further last-minute points arising, I should appreciate a telephone call to resolve them as speedily as possible.

Yours faithfully

25
Letter from architect to client, regarding amenity society objections

Dear

[*insert appropriate heading*]

I refer to our telephone conversation of [*insert date*] and confirm that you are in agreement with my suggestion that I should address the [*insert name of society*] members on the subject of the above proposals. The meeting will take place on [*insert date*] at [*insert time*] and I will report the result to you as soon as possible.

[*If your client has commodious premises and has agreed that the meeting should be held there, write the following instead:*]

I refer to our telephone conversation of [*insert date*] and confirm that you are in agreement with my suggestion that I should address [*insert name of society*] members at your premises on [*insert date*] at [*insert time*], the subject being the above project.

If you can arrange some light refreshments, a pleasant relaxed atmosphere should be possible in which we ought to be able to convince them that we share their concern for environmental issues.

Yours faithfully

26
Letter from architect to amenity society, if they have objections

Dear

[*insert appropriate heading*]

I refer to your letter of [*insert date*] and our telephone conversation of [*insert date*].

[*Add <u>one</u> of the following paragraphs:*]

I confirm that I will be delighted to attend a meeting of your members on [*insert date*] at [*insert time*] in the [*insert venue*] to speak and answer questions about the above project. I will bring illustrative material with me.

I confirm that a warm invitation is extended to your members, which I understand you accept, to visit my client's premises on [*insert date*] at [*insert time*] when I will speak and answer questions on the above project. Illustrative material will be on display. The address of my client's premises is [*insert address*]. Please let me know the approximate number you expect to attend.

Yours faithfully

D   Detailed Proposals

D1   Client, if no reply (27)

It may happen that, after you have produced your detailed proposals and presented them to your client for consideration and approval, you hear nothing for
some time. Exactly how long you should wait before taking some action depends
on circumstances. When you left your scheme, you should have requested a decision and obtained some idea of the time needed for consideration. For example,
there may be the need to discuss it with someone who is on holiday or to present
it to a meeting of the Board of Directors – although you should ask to present it
yourself at any such meeting.

   After taking everything into consideration, you may feel that your client
should have written or telephoned with either approval or comments. It is best
that you do not telephone without warning. An unexpected telephone call can
be unwelcome and provoke a hurried response. A letter is more likely to produce
a better reply, particularly if you make it clear that you intend to telephone later.

D2   Client, if another architect appointed to continue work (28), (29), (30)

Under the RIBA terms of appointment, the client is entitled to terminate your
appointment at any time if proper notice is given and any fees due are paid.
There are three important factors to consider:

● Whether the appointment is properly terminated
● Your copyright on the designs
● The appointment of another architect

   In general terms, the client will be entitled to use your designs provided you
have completed detailed proposals and all outstanding fees have been paid. If
one of the RIBA appointment documents has been used, you may have additional rights, depending upon whether SFA/99, CE/99 or SW/99 has been used.
If the client terminates your appointment prematurely, you may be entitled to
payment of some appropriate additional copyright licence fee.

   Depending on the circumstances if your client has not properly determined
under the terms of the appointment, it may amount to a repudiation for which

27
Letter from architect to client, if no reply

Dear

[insert appropriate heading]

We have reached an important stage in this project and I understand your wish to be certain that the scheme satisfies your requirements as fully as possible.

Much more preparatory work has to be done before operations can commence on site. If we can expedite this work, it should result, ultimately, in a lower contract price. At the moment, I am awaiting your comments on the detailed proposals which were left with you on *[insert date]*. May I ask you to let me have your approval or comments as soon as possible?

I will telephone in a day or so to discuss the current position.

Yours faithfully

you would be entitled to damages. This can be an extremely complicated situation and legal advice should be sought. The RIBA appointment documents contain clauses which permit either party to determine after giving proper notice, variously described as 'reasonable' or 'fourteen days'. If these documents or similar are not used or, if used, determination is not carried out under the relevant determination clauses, the client has probably repudiated, because the law does not allow a party to a contract to simply walk away at a whim. A repudiation on the part of your client entitles you to do one of two things:

(1)   Refuse to accept the repudiation, affirm the contract and claim whatever damages have been suffered; or
(2)   Accept the repudiation and claim damages

It is not always practicable to affirm and continue the contract, particularly if the client has appointed another architect to take your place. The acceptance of a repudiation strictly does not bring the contract to an end, but it does bring an end to your duties under the contract.

You should write to your client as soon as you are informed that your services are no longer required (**28**). If you simply hear that another architect has been appointed and you receive no communication from either client or architect (it does happen), you should write to both parties (**29**), (**30**).

D3   Client, if preference expressed for a particular sub-contractor (31)

If your client wishes to use a particular sub-contractor on a contract it usually implies nomination. Nomination is never a good idea if there is an alternative solution, because it tends to cause disputes. However, your client may insist or there may be no viable alternative. Nomination is no longer available under the JCT Standard Building Contract 2005 (SBC) although 'naming' through the JCT Intermediate Building Contract (IC and ICD) or through ACA 3 is still possible. It is not advisable to attempt nomination in some ad hoc way, for example through the JCT Minor Works Building Contract (MW and MWD).

Even if the sub-contractor is suitable, you might advise your client that it would be advisable to obtain competitive tenders. In practice, a good way out of the problem is to use clause 3.8 of SBC to create a list of a minimum of three suitable prospective sub-contractors. A problem arises if the sub-contractor is, in your opinion, unsuitable. There could be a number of reasons, among them:

- Too large or small to do the work
- Too inexperienced
- Your past experience has shown the sub-contractor to be unreliable or a poor operative

28
Letter from architect to client, under RIBA appointment if services terminated without proper notice

Dear

[*insert appropriate heading*]

Thank you for your letter of [*insert date*].

I note that you have terminated my services on the above project. In these circumstances, the appointment document requires you to give proper notice. In this instance you have neither given notice nor have you indicated that the termination is under the provisions of the appointment. I am advised that your actions amount to repudiatory breach of contract which I accept and I am entitled to recover damages for your breach.

I am arranging to stop all further work on your project as soon as possible. An account to cover all current outstanding fees is enclosed for your attention. As soon as I can reasonably so calculate, you will receive a note of the damage I have suffered as a result of the breach. When I receive payment, you will be entitled to all the drawings and documents prepared for the work although, due to the abruptness of the termination, the information will be incomplete and I cannot accept any responsibility for errors or omissions. It will be your responsibility to thoroughly check through and complete the production information or to get some other person to do it on your behalf.

[*continued*]

28 continued

[Add one of the following paragraphs: (A) if you have charged full recommended fees, (B) if you have charged a nominal fee:]

(A)   On payment of my fees, you are entitled to make use of the design, once only, on the site to which it relates. The copyright in all the documents remains my property.

(B)   You are not entitled to reproduce my designs by executing the project without my permission. I am prepared to grant you permission to reproduce my design, once only, on the site to which it relates on payment of an additional fee of £ *[insert amount]*. The copyright in all the documents remains my property.

Yours faithfully

29
Letter from architect to client, under RIBA appointment if another architect appointed

Dear

[*insert appropriate heading*]

I understand that you have appointed another architect to carry out the above project. Perhaps you would be good enough to confirm whether my information is correct?

My own appointment continues until you formally give me reasonable notice of termination. At that point I would prepare my fee account.

I look forward to hearing from you as soon as possible so that I can make the necessary preparations to stop work.

Yours faithfully

30
Letter from architect to another architect, appointed by client

Dear

[*insert appropriate heading*]

I have been informed that my client [*insert name*] has instructed you to carry out work on the above project. Since I have not had any communication from you, I should be pleased if you would let me know whether my information is correct.

I have also written to my client, informing him that my appointment is not terminated until I receive formal reasonable notice of termination, at which point I will submit my fee account.

I assume that you were not aware of my prior involvement but, if you already have accepted instructions, I should be grateful if you would inform my client that it would not be proper for you to proceed until the appropriate termination formalities have been completed.

Yours faithfully

31
Letter from architect to client, regarding unsuitable sub-contractor

Dear

[*insert appropriate heading*]

I refer to our discussion of [*insert date*] regarding the employment of [*insert name*] for sub-contract [*insert type of work*] works on the above contract and I confirm the following:

[*select appropriate points*]

1.   You instructed me to obtain competitive tenders from three firms including [*insert name*] for the above sub-contract works.

[*or*]

1.   You instructed me to obtain a tender from only one firm, [*insert name*], for the above sub-contract works.

[*then:*]

2.   I have advised you that, in my opinion, this/these firm(s) is/are not suitable for the work.
3.   I have further advised you that, if this firm/one of these firms was to get the work, the consequences to the contract could be far-reaching in terms of additional expense, delays in progress and completion and the quality of workmanship and materials.

[*continued*]

31 continued

4. If you insist, I will carry out your instructions but I can take no responsibility for the outcome because it is against my direct advice. You must understand that when the contract is signed, I must carry out my duty to administer the contract provisions fairly between the parties.

Please consider the matter once again and let me have your final instructions as soon as possible.

Yours faithfully

Your client should accept your advice, but that is not always the case (the sub-contractor may be a friend or relative). After using your powers of persuasion to no avail and warning of the possible consequences, confirm your views in writing to protect yourself in the future.

D4   Client: objection to the use of sub-contractor or supplier in a design capacity (32)

There is provision in SBC, MWD and ICD for the contractor to carry out design as the contractor's designed portion, but a sub-contractor or supplier is often used in a design capacity, for example as a named sub-contractor under IC or ICD, to design a lift installation. It is usual, in such cases, to arrange for a form of warranty to be completed. Naturally, the client must be informed of your intentions. There may be an objection on the grounds that you are supposed to be responsible for the design and additional fees are already being paid to consultants; therefore, surely all the design should be carried out by the professional advisors. You will have to write and explain. The principles, but not the precise wording in the letter, would apply if contractor design was involved.

32
Letter from architect to client, if there is an objection to a supplier or sub-contractor used in a design capacity

Dear

[*insert appropriate heading*]

Thank you for your letter of [*insert date*]. I can understand your concern and hasten to reassure you. The various consultants' fees are based only on the work they do. Therefore, any design work attributable to suppliers or to sub-contractors is excluded. I have proposed the present method of proceeding because the particular services offered by the supplier/sub-contractor [*omit as appropriate*] will be much cheaper than to commission a design by consultants and then have it carried out by the main contractor. This is because a number of suppliers/sub-contractors [*omit as appropriate*] have their own patented systems which they have refined over a number of years. There is a system of warranties and agreements to protect your interest in the event of a design failure.

I trust that I have allayed your fears and that you will signify your agreement to the employment of suppliers and sub-contractors [*use only one term if appropriate*] in a design capacity on this project.

Yours faithfully

E   Final Proposals

E1   Client: wishing to modify brief (33), (34)

Although you will have impressed upon your client the need for *final* briefing decisions at stage D, it is likely that some alterations will be requested at a later stage. 'Will you increase the car parking provisions from twenty to twenty-five cars?' is the sort of request which may be irritating but not catastrophic to the scheme as a whole. Late requests to alter the brief in a minor way are probably best acknowledged with a gentle reminder of timing (**33**). Alterations having a major effect require you to inform your client of the serious consequences. You must, as always, adjust the precise wording to suit the type of client. It should be remembered that it is not the architect's job to produce a never-ending series of designs until the client is satisfied (**34**). Most clients and many architects do not understand that, in accordance with the appointment, the architect undertakes to satisfy the client's brief, not the client's constantly changing brief. Provided that is done, the architect is entitled to charge for all subsequent changes.

33
Letter from architect to client, if minor modifications to the brief are required

Dear

[*insert appropriate heading*]

Thank you for your letter of [*insert date*] requesting me to [*insert a note of the alterations required*]. The work has been put in hand.

Although the alterations are minor, they will require a certain amount of redrawing, re-scheduling and liaison with consultants.

I know, from our previous conversations, that you appreciate the problems caused by quite small changes of mind and the repercussions in terms of additional fees, other costs and programme time. Obviously, the problems become more serious as the work of the design team progresses further.

Yours faithfully

Copy: Quantity surveyor

34
Letter from architect to client, if major modifications to the brief are required

Dear

[*insert appropriate heading*]

Thank you for your letter of [*insert date*] requesting me to [*insert a note of the alterations required*]. The work has been put in hand but your decision to change the brief at this late stage causes me concern on your behalf.

A considerable amount of work already completed must be amended, including liaison with consultants. It is now very unlikely that the date originally envisaged for commencement on site can be achieved.

I have asked the quantity surveyor to revise the cost estimates for you in the light of your latest requirements. Additional fees will be due to cover the extra work, and the consultants may also request additional fees.

May I very strongly reinforce what I have said in our previous conversations, that alterations in the brief at this stage can be very expensive in time and money? Obviously, as work progresses, alterations becoming increasingly time-consuming and costly.

Yours faithfully

Copy: Quantity surveyor

F   Production Information

F1   Client: declines to use a standard contract (35)

Your client may consider the JCT Standard Building Contract 2005 (SBC) excessively complicated and require you to use a simpler form of contract; possibly your client has a solicitor ready to draft an agreement. It may be that some variations of the standard contract, such as the Intermediate or the Minor Works Building Contract, would be appropriate, or it may be that a different procurement system is indicated, such as construction management or design and build. If so, try to persuade your client to use it. If not or if you are faced with a refusal, put the facts down in writing and consider whether you can administer the terms of an unknown contract without rendering yourself liable for any shortcomings.

F2   Client: wishes to use a partnering agreement without a legally binding contract (36)

Some clients have heard of partnering, but they do not understand the concept and naively believe that it is something which replaces a standard building contract with something altogether more client friendly. You should put the position in writing and probably follow up with a meeting to give a detailed exposition after your client has digested your letter.

F3   Client: wishes to include unsuitable contractor on tender list (37)

If your client asks you to include on the list of tenderers a contractor whom you know to be unsuitable, make the point very strongly. It is probably best to reserve your precise comments for oral communication. If your client insists, it might even be worthwhile relinquishing your commission rather than face the certainty of continuous dispute. It is too much to expect your client to thank you if you make a stand; but you will certainly be blamed later if you do not. Your letter is, to some extent, a variation of the letter in D3.

35
Letter from architect to a client who declines to use a standard contract

Dear

[*insert appropriate heading*]

I refer to our recent conversations regarding the use of the JCT Standard Building Contract (SBC). I appreciate that you find it long and complex and I understand why you think that a form of contract, drafted by your own solicitor, would be preferable. Before you come to a firm decision, however, I would ask you to consider the following:

1. The current standard building contracts were developed by the Joint Contracts Tribunal in 2005 after many years of experiencing the operation of the contract in practice. They are designed to cater for virtually every eventuality which might arise during the course of building Works of the kind you envisage.
2. The Joint Contracts Tribunal is composed of representatives of all sections of the building industry. As a result, the standard forms it produces are widely recognised throughout the industry and their implications are clearly understood by architect and contractor alike.
3. Contractors have a marked reluctance to tender other than on a standard form. JCT contracts are familiar to them and the use of a completely new form may well result in increased tender prices as contractors attempt to allow for the unknown. It is also possible that some contractors will refuse to tender.

[*continued*]

35 continued

4. It is part of my duty to understand the contract and interpret it fairly between the parties. I am familiar with the operation of the standard JCT contracts which not only set out the rights and obligations of the parties, but also form a set of procedures. I have no idea how your solicitor's proposed form would work. Indeed, if you insist on this unfamiliar and untried contract, I must consider whether I can continue to act for you.

I have to advise you about the most suitable form of contract for your purpose and to assist you in completion. If you have objections to specific parts, I will explain the implications to you. If you wish, I can obtain expert advice. This would be done best at a meeting and I will telephone you in a few days when you have had the opportunity to consider this letter.

Yours faithfully

36
Letter from architect to client, if client wants to use a partnering agreement without a legally binding contract

Dear

[*insert appropriate heading*]

I understand why you might wish to use a partnering agreement on this project. Whether it would be a good choice for this project is something which we can discuss later. However, I must correct one or two misunderstandings which seem to have arisen.

There are essentially two kinds of partnering scenario. The first involves the parties entering into a legally binding contract on a standard form in the usual way and at the same time putting their names to a non-binding partnering agreement (sometimes referred to as a 'partnering charter'). The second scenario has the parties entering into a special contract which combines some or all of the elements of a normal standard contract, but incorporates some of the key partnering principles, thereby giving legal force to these principles.

You will note that, in both scenarios, the parties are legally bound to one another and the important difference lies in the binding or non-binding nature of the partnering principles.

I look forward to meeting you to discuss this matter further and I will telephone shortly to arrange a mutually convenient time.

Yours faithfully

37
Letter from architect to client, if client wishes to include unsuitable contractor on tender list

Dear

[*insert appropriate heading*]

Thank you for your letter of [*insert date*]. I note that you wish me to include [*insert name*] on the tender list.

This contractor is well known to me and I do not consider it suitable to carry out the above work. I am, of course, prepared to explain my reasons more fully on the telephone or at a meeting. I trust, however, that it will not be necessary and you will confirm your agreement to exclude this particular contractor on this occasion.

Yours faithfully

F4   Client: asks you to recommend a contractor (38)

It may be suggested that your client understands nothing about building and that it would be best for you to recommend suitable contractors for inclusion on the tender list. Presumably you have carried out all the necessary checks and asked for references from other architects. Even though these checks may indicate that each of your proposed tenderers are firms of the highest calibre with impeccable financial pedigrees, you should on no account actually recommend any of them. You may face legal action for doing so if the contractor subsequently renders poor service. You cannot guarantee the contractor and you are not called upon to do so by your conditions of engagement.

F5   Client: reluctance to appoint a full-time clerk of works (39)

Your client may sometimes resist the appointment of a full-time clerk of works. It may be due to a failure to realise the significance of having constant inspection of certain jobs or just simply a distaste for the additional cost involved. Some large organisations have their own clerks of works permanently employed. In those cases, the organisation may not wish to commit a clerk of works full-time upon the site. The only alternative to a full-time clerk of works is a full-time architect, which would no doubt be even more expensive.

The employment of a full-time clerk of works will not relieve you of your obligations to your client. Indeed, an inefficient clerk of works could add to your difficulties, although a competent clerk of works is a boon. However, it is very much in your interests that your client does appoint a clerk of works, because it may reduce your liability for damages if the worst happens. However, if you recommend the appointment of a full-time clerk of works and your client is unwilling to agree, you should do what you can to safeguard your position.

MW, MWD

It is unusual for a clerk of works to be appointed, and there is no provision in the conditions. Provisions can be made for a clerk of works in the specification, however, if the size or complexity of the Works warrant it.

F6   Consultants, if late in supplying drawings and specification (40)

You are probably the design team leader and, if you want everything to be ready on time, you will have to be prepared to be tough. Each consultant is responsible to the client.

38
Letter from architect to client, if asked to recommend a contractor

Dear

[*insert appropriate heading*]

I refer to our recent telephone conversation when you asked me to recommend some contractors for inclusion on the tender list for this project.

Naturally, I will do everything I can to assist. Recommendation of contractors is not something which falls within the scope of my professional duties. What I can do is to carry out various checks in regard to financial standing and workmanship, including seeking references from other architects. I have carried out those checks in respect of the contractors listed on the attached sheet and the results are also enclosed. They indicate that each of the contractors appears capable of executing the Works to the required standard and you will note the remarks in the references I have obtained. The final decision must be yours, but I shall be happy to discuss your choices in the light of these results.

Perhaps you will telephone me when you have had the opportunity to consider the matter.

Yours faithfully

39
Letter from architect to client, if reluctant to appoint full-time clerk of works

Dear

[*insert appropriate heading*]

Thank you for your letter of [*insert date*] and I note that you think it unnecessary to appoint a full-time clerk of works upon the above contract.

In some contracts of limited value a clerk of works is clearly unnecessary. However, this contract does not fall into that category[1]. My conditions of engagement do not require me to be constantly on the site, but only to make visits and I strongly advise you to reconsider your decision. The employment of a clerk of works is likely to repay the cost several times over in savings on lost time and money as the contract progresses.

Although, naturally, I will carry out my own duties punctiliously, on a contract of this size[2] I cannot accept responsibility for failure to notice such defects as would be discovered by a full-time clerk of works.

Yours faithfully

[[1] *Omit the first two sentences of this paragraph when using MW or MWD.*
[2] *Substitute 'this type' when using MW or MWD.*]

40
Letter from architect to consultant, if information late

Dear

[*insert appropriate heading*]

According to the programme of work agreed by all members of the design team, you should have delivered [*indicate nature of information*] to this office on [*insert date*] at latest.

I telephoned [*insert name*] on [*insert date*] who promised to get the information to me by [*insert date*]. I have received nothing by this morning either in the post, by fax or e-mail.

The position now is that a substantial portion of my own work has been delayed by [*insert number of days or weeks*]. The consequences in cost and delay are unacceptable to our mutual client who will be looking to lay off my additional fees. I should be pleased to receive, by return, all programmed information and your assurance that no further delays will occur.

Yours faithfully

Copy: Client

You will have prepared a programme at a meeting of the design team so that all consultants know when their information is required. If some information from consultants is not available at the right time, you should lose no time in telephoning to hurry things along. Obtain a definite delivery promise. If the information is still delayed, confirm the situation in writing.

F7   Sub-contractor or supplier, if tender not on standard form or conditions attached (41), (42)

Named sub-contractors are rarely a good idea. There is much opportunity to make errors in completion of the documents and disputes often arise. If there is no alternative but to use named sub-contractors, you will have required tenders on the appropriate standard forms from all proposed named sub-contractors or suppliers. It is not unusual for either the standard form to be ignored and tenders to be submitted on the sub-contractor's own form, or for the standard form to be submitted with the firm's special conditions attached.

You cannot consider either tender. Basically, three courses of action are open to you:

- Exclude the tender from consideration
- Request the firm to resubmit on the proper form (**41**)
- Request the firm to withdraw their special condition (**42**)

F8   Sub-contractor or supplier, if price too high (43)

You may find that the lowest acceptable tender for a particular item of sub-contract or trade contract work or supply is higher than the estimate for this item in the overall cost plan prepared for the project. There can be many reasons for this, only one of which is an error in the initial estimate. If sufficient money can be found in other parts of the cost plan to make up the difference without the danger of lowering standards, there should be no problem, although it is always wise to inform your client that the tender exceeded the allowance.

Difficulties arise if the difference is too great and the total cost is likely to be increased. Do not attempt to cover up the problem. Your client will be disappointed but, most of all, will want advice. Give it clearly; your client may think the fault is yours. Be defensive and you will be confirming that the fault is yours.

In the letter you have carried out your duty exactly by informing your client, at the earliest possible moment, of the possibility of overspending. There is the opportunity to give you any fresh instructions your client may think appropriate. You have also confirmed that you are proceeding and, in effect, you are advising calm until the total main tender figure can be seen.

41
Letter from architect to sub-contractor or supplier, if tender improperly submitted (1)

Dear

[*insert appropriate heading*]

I have received your tender for [*insert type of work or materials*] in connection with the above contract. The tender cannot be considered in its present form. If you wish to be considered as a prospective named sub-contractor, please complete the standard form of tender, a further two copies of which are enclosed, and return it to me not later than [*insert date and time*].

Please note that the submission of the tender on your own form or the inclusion of your own special conditions, other than in the appropriate place on the standard form, will result in disqualification.

Yours faithfully

42
Letter from architect to sub-contractor or supplier, if tender improperly submitted (2)

Dear

[*insert appropriate heading*]

I have received your tender for [*insert type of work or materials*] in connection with the above contract.

If you wish your tender to be considered as a prospective named sub-contractor, you must inform me in writing by [*insert date*] that you withdraw the conditions [*specify conditions*] while maintaining your offer price of £ [*insert price in tender*] unchanged. If you do not feel able to agree to this course of action, your tender will not be considered.

Yours faithfully

43
Letter from architect to client, if sub-contractor's or supplier's price is too high

Dear

[*insert appropriate heading*]

We have received tenders for [*indicate the item of work*]. The lowest acceptable tender amounted to [*state the sum*]. The sum allowed in the cost plan was [*state the sum*]. The difference is greater than the total savings on the rest of the prime cost sums by a margin of [*state the sum*]. In my opinion we are unlikely to achieve a lower price by inviting new tenders. At this stage the indication is that the total estimate for the Works will be exceeded by [*state the sum*]. Obviously, it is not possible to say what the lowest tender figure for the main contract will be.

To attempt to achieve savings at this stage may be misguided because some lowering of standards would be involved which could prove to be unnecessary. Unless you instruct me to the contrary, therefore, I will proceed with my work, and, when the main contract tenders are received, we can review the situation together if the estimated total cost is exceeded.

Yours faithfully

Copy: Quantity surveyor

F9 Letters of intent to sub-contractors or suppliers (44)

You may feel that it is desirable to have named sub-contract design carried out, to have shop drawings produced or even to put certain work in hand before the main contract is let. The procedure is usually carried out by means of a letter of intent. The process is fraught with difficulties:

- The main contractor, when appointed, may object to the particular sub-contractor unless it has been named in the main contract tender documents
- The client will be faced with certain costs even if the project does not proceed
- Letters of intent have sometimes been found to create a full binding contract
- If the whole, or substantially the whole, of the sub-contract work is carried out on the basis of a letter of intent, the sub-contractor may be entitled to payment on the basis of *quantum meruit* (a reasonable sum – defined as a 'fair commercial rate'). It could amount to considerably more than the sub-contract tender figure, particularly in times of keen tendering.

The inescapable conclusion is that letters of intent should be avoided. If you must send one, make sure that your client has approved in writing and is fully aware of the implications. Your letter must be seen by your client who must agree its terms before you send it. It is probably not going too far to suggest that every letter of intent should be scrutinised by an expert contract consultant before being despatched.

44
Letter from architect to sub-contractor or supplier: letter of intent

Dear

[*insert appropriate heading*]

My client, [*insert name*], has instructed me to inform you that your tender of the [*insert date*] in the sum of [*insert amount in figures and words*] for [*insert the nature of the works or materials*] is acceptable and that I intend to instruct the main contractor to enter into a sub-contract[1] with you after the main contract has been signed.

It is not my client's intention that this letter, taken alone or in conjunction with your tender, should form a binding contract. However, my client is prepared to instruct you to [*insert the limited nature of the work or materials required*]. If, for any reason whatsoever, the project does not proceed, my client's commitment will be strictly limited to payment for [*insert the limited nature of the work or materials required*].

No other work[2] included in your tender must be carried out[3] without further written order. No further obligation is placed upon my client and no obligation whatever, under any circumstances, is placed upon me.

Yours faithfully

[[1] *Substitute 'place an order' in the case of a supplier.*
[2] *Substitute 'materials' in the case of a supplier.*
[3] *Substitute 'supplied' in the case of a supplier.*]

G   Bills of Quantities

Note: This section will not be required if it is proposed to use SBC, IC or ICD Without Quantities, MW or MWD.

G1   Drawings, if not ready

The quantity surveyor requires all drawings and other production information to be complete before beginning to take off quantities. In practice, it very rarely works out so smoothly and the quantity surveyor usually starts work before all drawings are finished, and problems occur if amendments are made. The quantity surveyor, understandably, can become frustrated.

If your production information is not complete or not sufficiently complete for the quantity surveyor to commence an uninterrupted sequence of taking off, you have only two courses of action open to you:

- Send what you have and follow up with the remainder of the information as quickly as possible in the hope that you can somehow keep the quantity surveyor with enough information to keep going
- Inform the quantity surveyor, as far in advance as possible, that you will not be able to deliver sufficient information by the appointed date and state a new date by which sufficient information can be ready

The first course, even if the quantity surveyor co-operates to the fullest, is a recipe for disaster because you will be bombarded with queries to such an extent that you will be unable to make adequate progress on the production information still outstanding. It is likely that the bills of quantities will be delayed and, more seriously, mistakes will occur.

If you set back the date one or two weeks, you will lose little; the quantity surveyor may even be able to recover some of the delay. The chances of mistakes will be reduced and your relationship will not be soured before the contract begins. Indeed, you may make a friend by your willingness to state that you are not ready and your confident naming of a new date.

G2   Bills of quantities, if behind programme (45), (46)

You may find that the quantity surveyor falls behind the programme, although you have co-ordinated all necessary information and delivered it in good time. You may be notified that the date for completion of the bills of quantities ready for sending out to tender must be put back.

Obviously, any delay tends to increase the tender sums. At some point during this stage you will have confirmed the list of tenderers and given them an indication of the date they can expect to receive the tender documents. In turn, they will have programmed the complex and expensive tendering process into their other work. Clearly, a delay can cause disruption to some contractors, depending upon the amount of work they have on their books. It may even mean that one or two contractors have to withdraw.

The sooner the quantity surveyor informs you that the date cannot be met the better, so that you can notify the contractors (**45**) and, if necessary, choose new firms to replace any who withdraw. It is no use berating the quantity surveyor at this stage. The best laid plans go astray. It does no harm, however, to let him or her know that you will expect their help in keeping the cost down (**46**).

45
Letter from architect to all contractors on tender list, if quantity surveyor behind programme

Dear

[*insert appropriate heading*]

I refer to my letter of [*insert date*] informing you that you had been included on the tender list of the above project and advising you of the provisional date when you could expect to receive the tender documents.

Unforeseen circumstances have caused a reassessment of that date and I expect to despatch the documents on [*insert date*].

Please check your programme of work and confirm, by return if possible, that you still wish, and will be able, to submit a tender in accordance with the revised dates.

Yours faithfully

Copy: Quantity surveyor

46
Letter from architect to quantity surveyor, if behind programme

Dear

[*insert appropriate heading*]

Thank you for your letter of [*insert date*] from which I note that you do not expect to be in a position to finalise the bills of quantities until [*insert date*]. This will be [*insert number*] weeks after the programmed date. It is unfortunate but we will have to make the best of it if there is no possibility of any improvement.

I have informed all the firms on the tender list that the tender documents will be delayed by approximately [*insert number*] weeks. Some firms may find themselves unable to tender because of other commitments and, in any case, the result may be a generally higher set of tenders. I do not think it is practicable or wise to try to cut down the tender period.

I know that you feel responsible for the situation but, equally, I know that I can rely upon you to help in negotiating a reduction in the lowest tender if it should prove necessary.

Yours faithfully

Copy: Client

H   Tender Action

H1   Client, if he wishes to accept the lowest, but unsatisfactory, tender (47)

It is normal good practice to open all tenders in the presence of your client. If there are no irregularities, usually the lowest tender is approved for acceptance.

It is assumed that the *Code of Practice for the Selection of Main Contractors* developed by the Construction Industry Board has been adopted. When contractors respond to an invitation to tender on this or any other basis, your client is undertaking to carry out the procedures correctly and failure to do so may result in a contractor seeking damages for breach of the agreement. Tender forms which are amended or qualified should be rejected if the tenderer has refused the opportunity to withdraw the qualification without amendment to the tender.

Difficulties arise if your client wishes to accept a qualified tender which is the lowest by a substantial margin. A client may care little for the Code of Practice and look purely at the economics. Indeed, the qualifications, in retrospect, may be quite sensible. It is also common for clients to wish to open and consider a late tender. You should make clear to the client that such conduct is not an option. The tendering process places legal obligations upon the client, breach of which may result in a claim for substantial damages from all tenderers. It is advisable to put your advice in writing so that there is no doubt in the future.

Obviously your professional integrity is also at stake, but it may not be advisable to mention it at this stage. Stick to the points your client will appreciate. If your letter fails to make any impression, you must seriously consider whether you wish to continue to be associated with the project. You can inform your client of your professional position at that point.

47
Letter from architect to a client who wishes to accept the lowest but irregular tender

Dear Sir

[*insert appropriate heading*]

Following the meeting today at which tenders were opened, I should confirm the points I made so that you can give them proper consideration.

1. All tenderers were informed that the tendering procedure would be in accordance with the *Code of Practice for the Selection of Main Contractors*. Each contractor, by submitting a tender on that basis, has entered into a small contract with you under which you are obliged to strictly adhere to the principles in the code in considering tenders. Failure to do so may result in an action for damages by one or more of the unsuccessful contractors.

2. A tenderer who amends the tender form, adds qualifications or submits a late tender is clearly seeking to gain an unfair advantage. As you know, [*insert name of firm*] was unwilling to withdraw its qualifications without amendment to its tender figure. If all tenderers had been given carte blanche to qualify their tenders as they thought fit, any yardstick for judging one firm against another would have vanished. If late tenders are accepted, there is simply no point in going through a tendering process.

3. All other considerations apart, the adoption of a widely recognised system of tendering has a beneficial effect upon the whole construction industry in keeping prices down.

[*continued*]

47 continued

The irregular tender submitted by [*insert name*] should be rejected and the lowest properly submitted tender be subjected to the usual checking procedure. If no problems are encountered, I would be prepared to negotiate with the assistance of the quantity surveyor with the object of achieving a lower contract figure which could be accepted.

Please let me have your instructions as soon as possible.

Yours faithfully

Copy: Quantity surveyor

J Mobilisation

J1 Clerk of works: letter of instruction (48)

It is imperative that, when appointed, the clerk of works knows precisely what is expected. If you have worked together before, the situation is obviously better than that when an unfamiliar clerk of works is employed. In either case you should send a brief letter of instruction before work commences on site. Most firms have evolved their own report form and it would be superfluous to illustrate yet another.

MW, MWD

There is no provision for a clerk of works in the conditions but you may have made provision in the specification, possibly in terms similar to clause 3.3 of IC or ICD. If so, this section is applicable.

J2 Letter of intent: contractor (49)

The general remarks regarding a letter of intent to sub-contractor and supplier apply to any letter of intent to the main contractor.

The occasions when such a letter has to be written should be rare, but some organisations have such ponderous administrative systems that they require a letter of intent to get things moving while necessary approvals are obtained and the formal contract is being prepared. A danger for your client is that a formal contract may never be executed and the contractor can leave site and abandon the Works at any time, leaving your client without a remedy. In this situation, the contractor would be entitled to payment on a *quantum meruit* basis, which may be greater than the contract rates. If a letter of intent is to be sent, great care must be taken to create only a limited contract at this stage. You need the contractor to do enough so that the whole project is not unduly delayed. Whether the contractor is prepared to operate on this basis is another matter. Your letter will be so guarded that you must not be surprised if the contractor rejects it.

48
Letter from architect to clerk of works, giving instructions

Dear Sir

[*insert appropriate heading*]

My client, [*insert name*], has confirmed your appointment as clerk of works for the above contract. I should be pleased if you would call at this office on [*insert date*] at [*insert time*] to be briefed on the project and to collect your copies of drawings, schedules, bills of quantities/specification, weekly report forms, site diary and pad of direction forms [*delete as applicable*].

The contractor is expected to take possession of the site on [*insert date*]. You will be expected to be present on site [*insert periods during which the clerk of works is expected to be present*]. Let me know at the end of the first week if proper accommodation is not provided for you as described in the bills of quantities/specification [*delete as applicable*].

Your duties will be as indicated in the conditions of contract clause 3.4/3.3/specification [*delete as applicable*], a copy of which is enclosed for your reference. I wish to draw your attention to the following:

[*continued*]

---

48 continued

---

1. You will be expected to inspect all workmanship and materials to ensure conformity with the contract, i.e. the drawings, schedules, bills of quantities/specification/employer's requirements [*delete as applicable*] and any further information and instructions issued from this office. Any defects must be pointed out to the person-in-charge, to whom you should address all comments. If any defects are left unremedied for twenty-four hours or if they are of a major or fundamental nature, you must let me know immediately by telephone.

2. The contract does not empower you to mark defective work on site, although I am aware that it is common practice. You must not in any way deface materials on site whether or not they are incorporated into the structure.

3. It is not my policy to issue lists of defects to the contractor before practical completion. Commonly called snagging lists, they may be misinterpreted and give rise to disputes. Any lists of defects required should be produced by the person-in-charge. Please confine your remarks to the contractor to oral comments.

4. The architect is the only person empowered to issue instructions to the contractor.

5. Any queries, unless of a minor explanatory nature, should be referred to me for decision. You are not empowered to issue any instructions varying, adding or omitting work.

6. The report sheets must be filled in completely and a copy sent to me on Monday of each week. Pay particular attention to listing all visitors to site, the state of the weather and commenting on work done in as much detail as possible.

7. The diary is provided for you to enter up your daily comments.

8. Remember that your weekly reports and site diary may be called in evidence should a dispute arise so you must bear this in mind when making your entries and refrain from comments of a personal nature and from the use of unnecessary or extreme epithets.

[*continued*]

---

48 continued

[Add the following item if appropriate:]

9.   I intend to make you my authorised representative for the purpose of
     verifying daywork sheets and for that purpose alone. Do not sign any
     sheets submitted later than the end of the week following the week in
     which work has been carried out nor any sheets which are not
     factually accurate.

The successful completion of the contract depends in large measure upon
your relationship with the contractor. If you are in any doubt upon
anything please let me know.

Yours faithfully

49
Letter from architect to contractor: letter of intent

Dear Sir

[*insert appropriate heading*]

My client [*insert name*], has instructed me to inform you that your tender of [*insert date*] in the sum of [*insert amount in figures and words*] for the above project is acceptable and that, subject to my client [*insert the provisos appropriate to the particular situation*], I intend to prepare the main contract documents for signature.

It is not my client's intention that this letter, taken alone or in conjunction with your tender, should form a binding contract. However, my client is prepared to instruct you to [*insert the limited nature of the work required*].

If, for any reason whatsoever, the project does not proceed, my client's commitment will be strictly limited to payment for [*insert the limited nature of the work required*]. No other work included in your tender must be carried out without a further written order. No further obligation is placed upon my client and no obligation whatever, under any circumstances, is placed upon me.

Yours faithfully

J3   Consents: not received from planning authority (50), building control (51), (52), statutory undertakings (53)

If you discover, at this stage, that you have not obtained one of the necessary consents, your position is awkward. You will wish to avoid a delay which could cost money and which your client will look to recover; probably from you. Even worse, if a consent is now refused, major redesign and re-tendering could result. It is convenient to deal with the major consents one at a time.

Planning authority

The reasons for not obtaining a consent are basically:

● You have not applied for one
● You have applied but a problem has delayed receipt

If you have not applied, clearly you must apply immediately. Eight weeks (thirteen weeks if it is a major development) are allowed for a decision unless the planning authority agreed with you to extend the time for making a decision. If you do not agree to an extension, the planning authority will make a decision on the application as it stands at that time. Failure to make a decision does not imply anything, although you can appeal.

Simple applications are often decided well within the period. You will be conscious of:

● The period the lowest tender remains open for acceptance (usually three months)
● The attitude likely to be adopted by your client
● Any aspects of your scheme likely to be considered contentious by the planning authority

You should present your application personally and explain the situation to the planning officer – the chief planning officer if possible. Make absolutely sure that your project is going to be recommended for approval. This may take time because, if the scheme is any size at all, the planning authority will carry out extensive consultations with a large number of other authorities and they may require revisions. Do not attempt to commence work on site until approval has been obtained. The legal consequences can be dire and, in any case, you will not endear yourself to the planning authority.

Although the planning authority have to go through all the proper motions in considering an application, they will usually try their best to speed things up as much as possible provided you play fair with them. You should also notify your client (see letter **50**).

If you have made an application already and you have not yet received approval, telephone the planning authority immediately and explain your

50
Letter from architect to client, if planning consent not obtained

Dear Sir

[*insert appropriate heading*]

[*First sentence optional depending on circumstances.*]

Checks on the lowest tender have been carried out and it has been found to be acceptable.

In carrying out my own checks prior to arranging a start on site, I note that planning consent has not been obtained. Work on site cannot commence before approval has been given. The lowest tender remains open for acceptance until [*insert date*] and, therefore, I do not propose to notify your acceptance to the contractor until I have planning approval.

I am pressing the planning authority to give approval as soon as possible and I shall let you know as soon as there is further news.

Yours faithfully

difficulty. There will be a reason why you have not received approval and it is essential that you sort out the problem without delay. How long it will take to receive approval will then depend on the authority. You may be tempted to stall for time with your client. Unless you are sure that approval is to be given within days, stalling is bad policy as far as your client is concerned. He or she is entitled to know that the contract may be delayed.

Your letter may not satisfy your client but, although you may be considered careless (at the least), you have carried out your duty as soon as the situation became clear to you. You have not attempted to hide the facts and your client should appreciate that. If not, a personal meeting is indicated at which you can explain the position. You have made a serious mistake but you are not covering up and possibly making matters worse.

Building control

The reasons for not receiving building regulations approval are the same as for planning approval. If you have not applied, do so immediately. Take the documents along personally and go through them with the building control officer to make sure that they are in order. There is a mandatory requirement to make an application by way of at least two days' clear notice. This may be in the form of 'full plans', 'building notice', or 'initial notice' submitted by an approved inspector. It is not necessary to get approval before commencing work. It is usual practice in such circumstances for building control to write stating that your client may proceed at own risk pending approval of your application. Confirm the position to Building Control and let your client know (**51**), (**52**).

Of course you must be sure that your building does conform to the regulations in every respect before you send such a letter. If you have already communicated acceptance to the lowest tenderer, you must adjust the letter accordingly and then you have little alternative but to proceed on site. In such circumstances, where a notice has not yet been given, the quickest option is to submit a building notice. There is no formal approval of plans by the authority and work can proceed after two days.

If you have already made an application under the traditional system, you should receive a decision within five weeks unless the authority obtains your permission to extend the period. If you do not receive a decision or a request to extend the time, the local authority is in breach of its duty and must refund the fee. There is no deemed approval. The operative date will have been notified to you immediately after your application has been received. If the authority requests an extension, it will be for your benefit since it implies that your application is not acceptable in its present state. If you refuse an extension, the application will be refused.

51
Letter from architect to building control, if application late

Dear Sir

[*insert appropriate heading*]

I refer to the meeting with your [*insert name*] on [*insert date*] when I deposited all the required documents to support an application for approval under the building regulations. I understand that, subject to your detailed checking, the information supplied is likely to be satisfactory.

Work on site is scheduled to commence on [*insert date*]. [*If the traditional system of deposit of full plans is being used add the following:*] I trust that formal approval will be notified very shortly thereafter, but until it is received my client understands that it will be proceeding on site at its own risk.

Yours faithfully

Copy: Client

52
Letter from architect to client, if building regulations approval not obtained and full plans deposited under the traditional system

Dear Sir

[*insert appropriate heading*]

Approval under the building regulations has not yet been obtained for the above project. A start may be made on site at your own risk, i.e. if any work is found to be not in accordance with the building regulations, it would have to be corrected. I am as confident as it is reasonable to be that all the drawings conform with the regulations. Alternatively, the lowest tender need not be accepted until [*insert date*] and you may wish to wait. Approval will take up to five weeks.

Please let me have your instructions.

Yours faithfully

Statutory undertakings (53)

The various statutory undertakings, principally gas, water and electricity suppliers, should have been consulted early in the project. They have certain obligations to supply services subject to the distance of your project from the mains. Any serious problems are likely to be encountered:

● In an entry to the building
● If you require a diversion of the existing mains or services

The requirements for service entry to buildings are generally well known and it is unusual for difficulties to arise if you have sent copies of your drawings to the appropriate suppliers so that they can indicate any special requirements. If you have forgotten to do that, take your drawings along by hand, discuss your service requirements and then confirm in writing.

A proposed diversion should be sorted out with the appropriate supplier at the earliest possible moment. If you have forgotten to do that, you should contact the supplier and discuss the problem. Assuming that a diversion is possible, the biggest difficulty is likely to be the cost. Statutory undertakings are normally prepared to give an estimate but nothing approaching a firm price. You will not know until after the work of each supplier is complete, including any diversions, what the final price will be. Therefore, there appears to be no good reason to worry your client with a report of the estimated cost of a late diversion unless it is likely to be very large. It is worth bearing in mind that, if the problem is simply that you have not already agreed a diversion with the supplier, the cost of the diversion will be the same as if you had previously agreed it. Any additional cost will be related to delays to the Works.

53
Letter from architect to statutory undertaking, if late in requesting entry details

Dear Sir

[*insert appropriate heading*]

I refer to my visit to your office on [*insert date*] when I discussed the service requirements for the above project with [*insert name*].

I understand that you anticipate no difficulties in servicing and carrying out your work to conform with the main contractor's programme. I will ask him to contact you as soon as he is appointed.

I confirm that work is expected to commence on site on [*insert date*] and I understand that you will return my drawings with your services indicated thereon within the next few days.

Yours faithfully

K Construction to Practical Completion

K1 Commencement before formal contract (54), (55)

A frequent source of difficulty is the fact that the contractor wishes to start on site before the formal contract has been signed. Sometimes it is the employer who is anxious for the work to proceed as quickly as possible. If the contract documents are signed within a few days of the contractor taking possession of the site, it is doubtful whether there will be any side effects. However, if signing is delayed for several weeks, the contractor and the employer may find themselves asking the following questions:

- Is there any problem with regard to certification of monies due?
- Can *any* of the provisions of the formal contract be put into effect?
- What is the position if the employer or contractor decides to bring the project to an end after possession of the site but before signing?

The answers to all these questions will depend on:

- Whether a contract exists
- Whether a contract exists which incorporates the terms of the formal documents

The contractor will have been chosen usually from a group of tenderers, either because the price was lowest or for some other good reason. The tender will have been on the basis of bills of quantities, schedules of work, or specification and drawings. Since a contract is made by an offer, acceptance and consideration, everything depends upon the wording of the letter of acceptance from the employer (or from the architect on the employer's behalf) to the contractor, which must be unequivocal and not subject to anything if it is to be effective (54).

An unequivocal letter of acceptance will form a valid binding contract leaving no room for doubt, and there is no difficulty in applying the provisions of the formal contract because they will have been referred to in the bills of quantities, schedules of work, or specification which form part of the basis of the contractor's tender and, therefore, they will have been incorporated. It follows, therefore, that neither side can put an end to the contract without severe legal repercussions.

54
Letter from architect to contractor accepting tender (correct version)

Dear

[*insert appropriate heading*]

My client, [*insert name*], has instructed me to inform you that your tender dated [*insert date*] is accepted in the sum of [*insert sum in words*] for the above work in accordance with drawings numbered [*insert numbers*] and the bills of quantities, schedules of work, specification [*delete as applicable*].

In response to your request, my client informs me that you will be allowed to take possession of the site on [*insert date*] and, consequently, the date for completion will be [*insert date*].

The contract documents are being prepared on this basis and will be forwarded to you for signature as soon as possible.

Yours faithfully

If it is not possible to give the contractor an unequivocal acceptance of the tender, perhaps because the employer will only accept if there are some changes, the contractor should submit another tender incorporating details of the changes so that you can unequivocally accept the revised tender on behalf of the employer and form a binding contract as noted earlier. If you simply attempt to accept a tender and make the acceptance subject to the changes required by the employer, there will be no binding contract until the contractor has written back and accepted the proposed changes. In practice, what tends to happen in these cases is that the contractor writes back and accepts some, but not all the changes and still there is no contract. The outcome of this situation is that either, several exchanges of correspondence later, full agreement occurs or there is never full agreement and the parties proceed with the Works without a binding contract although neither may realise it; both fondly imagining that they are proceeding on the basis of what they have put forward. This is a recipe for disputes.

It is extremely doubtful whether letter **55** will complete a valid binding contract because it is an acceptance subject to further agreement. Generally, if the words 'subject to' appear in such a letter the result is that there is no contract incorporating the terms of the formal documents until the further agreement has been made and no provisions of the formal contract can be put into effect. There may be a contract of some kind based on conduct, but the terms are doubtful and certainly not those of the formal contract documents, which are expressly excluded until the agreement and signing takes place. If, following the letter, the contractor begins work but the formal documents are not agreed or signed, the amount payable to the contractor is uncertain and there are no terms covering, for example, instructions and variations, extensions of time, loss and/or expense or termination. Alternatively, there may be no contract at all and the contractor may be entitled to a reasonable sum for work done. In such a situation, either party may simply bring the work to an end without serious penalty. The precise position depends upon the particular facts. Legal advice should be sought and the law reports show that even the courts have difficulty in these situations. The golden rule is never to allow a start on site before the formal documents are signed unless a very clear letter of acceptance is sent.

K2   Contract documents: initials missing (56)

Deletions or additions to the conditions must be initialled by both parties, preferably at the beginning and end of each such amendment.

More often than one cares to admit, a set of initials is missed. Experience shows that this most often occurs as a mistake by the employer. If the amendment is clearly the intention of the parties as evidenced by the bills of quantities, schedules of work, or specification, it is probably best to let the matter lie provided that it does not attempt to override or modify the printed conditions. Clause 1.3 of SBC, IC and ICD and clause 1.2 of MW and MWD expressly prevent such overriding or modification. If the amendment is evidenced in the bills, schedules

55
Letter from architect to contractor accepting tender (incorrect version)

Dear

[*insert appropriate heading*]

My client, [*insert name*], has instructed me to inform you that your tender dated [*insert date*] is accepted in the sum of [*insert sum in words*] for the above work in accordance with the drawings numbered [*insert numbers*] and the bills of quantities/schedule of work/specification [*delete as appropriate*] subject to the agreement and signing of the formal contract documents. They will be forwarded to you as soon as possible for your agreement and signature.

In response to your request, my client instructs me that you will be allowed to take possession of the site on [*insert date*] and, consequently, the date for completion will be [*insert date*].

Yours faithfully

56
Letter from architect to client or contractor (depending on whose initials are missing), to initial an amendment

Dear

[*insert appropriate heading*]

It has been drawn to my attention that you have omitted to initial one of the agreed amendments to the conditions of contract. In order to rectify the matter it would be appreciated if you would ask [*insert name of the person who originally signed the document*] to telephone me to arrange a mutually suitable time to correct the omission.

Yours faithfully

or specification but conflicts with the printed conditions or if it is the result of negotiation (perhaps oral) before acceptance of the tender, the matter is more serious. It is then vital that the amendment is initialled as evidence of what the parties intend.

What the parties intended at the beginning is often, as we all know, different from what they wish they had intended later in the contract. In that case it is better to get the difficulty sorted out earlier rather than later.

Note that in any letter it is inadvisable to specify the precise amendment because the result might be that whoever originally signed will give the matter considerable thought and decide that the amendment was ill-judged. On the other hand, if the document is simply presented for initialling, it is more than likely the amendment will be recognised as one which was agreed and it will be initialled accordingly. There is nothing wrong or devious in doing things this way since you are only concerned with correcting a clear oversight, but doing it in a way which recognises the vagaries of human nature.

K3   Contract documents: drawings amended (57), (58)

When the contract drawings have been prepared for sending out to tender, it is essential to keep the originals so that they will be available to generate more copies for inclusion in the contract documents. If, as is likely, the drawings have been produced by CAD, a disk containing the appropriate data must be set safely on one side.

If one of these procedures is not adopted, it is probable that the original drawings will have undergone some revision before the formal contract is signed. You will be faced with the task of altering the drawings back to their original state before incorporating them in the formal contract. Some confusion is certain to result. It is crucial that the drawings with the invitation to tender and the drawings in the formal contract are identical, otherwise the contract documents will not represent what the contractor undertook to do for the tender price and dispute will almost certainly result. This is extremely important where quantities are not part of the contract.

If you forget, there is no real alternative but to alter the drawings as soon as you discover your mistake and invite both contractor and client to sign them again. It is best that no time is wasted so do not simply send the drawings or ask the client or contractor to call around to your office some time. Recognise that it is your fault and be prepared to take some trouble to put matters right.

K4   Drawings, schedules: not ready (59), (60)

It is your responsibility to ensure that the contractor has two copies of 'any descriptive schedules or similar documents necessary for use in carrying out the Works (excluding CDP Works)' (clause 2.9.1.1) and you must provide them 'as

57
Letter from architect inviting contractor to re-sign new contract drawings

Dear

[*insert appropriate heading*]

On perusal of the signed contract drawings, it is clear that numbers [*insert numbers of defective drawings*] do not correspond precisely with the drawings on which you tendered because later amendments were incorporated.

In order to ensure a proper record of the contract, I have prepared a new set of drawings, altered back to their original state, and propose calling on you at [*insert time*] on [*insert date*] so that you can satisfy yourself that the new set are identical with those on which you tendered, and sign them. I will bring a spare set for your retention. Please let me know if the time suggested is convenient.

Yours faithfully

58
Letter from architect inviting client to re-sign new contract drawings

Dear

[*insert appropriate heading*]

On perusal of the signed contract drawings, it is clear that numbers [*insert numbers of defective drawings*] do not correspond precisely with the drawings on which the contractor tendered because later amendments were incorporated.

In order to ensure a proper record of the contract, I have prepared a new set of drawings altered back to their original state and propose calling on you at [*insert time*] on [*insert date*] so that you can add your signature to that of the contractor which I have already obtained. Please let me know if the time suggested is inconvenient.

Yours faithfully

soon as possible after the execution of this Contract' (clause 2.9.1). It is not entirely clear what is intended by this clause. Obviously, it does not refer to all the detailed drawings which the architect will need to issue under clause 2.12 and for which the contract sets out a detailed (clause 2.11) and a general (clause 2.12) programme. It is suggested that 'descriptive schedules' should be read literally and that 'similar documents' means simply other schedules and lists.

It seems that information release schedules as envisaged under clause 2.11 are not often used. In the absence of an information release schedule, your obligation is to issue drawings and information under clause 2.12 as necessary to amplify the contract documents and allow the contractor to complete by the contract completion date. If, however, the contractor is running late, you can tailor the issue of drawings to suit. That may not be a good idea, because it will be difficult to demonstrate later if the contractor argues that your late drawings caused slow progress on site rather than the reverse. However, you do not have to issue drawings early to suit the contractor's wish to finish early.

The contractor sometimes tries to gain an advantage by making application for all the drawings immediately the contract is signed. The contractor often threatens unspecified claims for extension of time and loss and/or expense.

Of course, every contractor would like to have all the information it needs to build right at the beginning of the job. The contract, however, provides for the realities. Most contractors appreciate the fact. Some, as noted earlier, will try to make capital out of the situation.

The first thing for you to do is to check that the contractor has got everything immediately needed for building or ordering purposes. It is to some extent a subjective test, which you must try to carry out as fairly as possible. Assuming that you are happy that the contractor has all the drawings reasonably required, you should answer the contractor's claims (**59**).

IC, ICD

The position is similar but this contract sensibly does not have an equivalent to clause 2.9.1 of SBC referring to 'descriptive schedules' being issued as soon as possible after the execution of the contract. Clauses 2.10 and 2.11 are very similar to clauses 2.11 and 2.12 respectively of SBC. Reference to extension of time and loss and/or expense for late delivery of information is contained in clauses 2.20.6 and 4.18.5 respectively.

MW, MWD

There is no reference to claims for loss and/or expense other than in a limited way as a result of carrying out architects' instructions (AI) requiring variations in clause 3.6, but that does not mean that the contractor will not make any claims. Any such claims would have to be referred to the employer for a decision. The letter should serve four purposes:

59
Letter from architect to contractor, if all drawings are not available

Dear

[*insert appropriate heading*]

Thank you for your letter of [*insert date*].

If you wish to persist in your claim perhaps you will let me have full supporting information.

Quite frankly, however, I think that you are premature. I confirm that, in my opinion, you have all the information reasonably necessary for you to proceed with the Works.

Having said that, I do welcome any selective requests for specific information made in good time. Indeed, that is your duty under clause 5.4.2.[1] Such a procedure is of mutual benefit. I will be sending you further details from time to time but do please let me know if there is any particular drawing you require within the next week.

Yours faithfully

[[1] *Substitute '1.7.2' when using IC or ICD.*]

- It should show your willingness to examine any properly presented claim
- It should gently let the contractor know that his current claim is recognised as a device only
- It should confirm that all necessary drawings have been handed over
- It should indicate the desire to co-operate in a logical sequence of information provision. It is always best to agree a series of dates with the contractor so that drawings can be supplied at the right time

The problem really occurs if the contractor is correct and all the information needed has not been provided. You will have a good idea what is missing and, no doubt, all available staff will be working on the project. You can either admit that the information is not ready and brace yourself for the inevitable claim or you can attempt to defuse the situation and buy a little time (**60**).

In order to substantiate a claim that all necessary drawings should have been received at the beginning of the contract, it will be necessary for the contractor to indicate the drawings required and state why each one is needed. That is a formidable task. Rather than expend time and energy producing such a claim, which would be the subject of much argument, the contractor may opt for the easy way out by simply naming the priority drawings. The contractor is unlikely to want to jeopardise relations on the whole contract at the very beginning if matters can be settled quickly so that progress can be maintained. Presumably that is your view also.

K5   Failure to give possession on the due date (61)

If the employer fails to give possession on the date noted in the contract particulars, the difficulty can usually be remedied by the employer deferring the giving of possession provided the appropriate clause (2.5) is stated in the contract particulars to apply. The deferment period must not exceed six weeks or whatever lesser period is stated in the contract particulars. Clearly, the earlier the employer can notify the contractor the better. Deferment will entitle the contractor to an extension of time under clause 2.29.3; indeed you must grant such extension if the employer is not to lose the right to deduct liquidated damages for the contractor's own delays. Deferment will also entitle the contractor to make application for reimbursement of loss and/or expense under clause 4.23 and, therefore, the greater the notice which can be given, the easier it is for the contractor to mitigate any losses. It is, of course, possible to amend the deferment period in the contract particulars and also clause 2.5 to allow a period in excess of six weeks, but no doubt an increased period would be reflected in the tender price as inserting a large element of uncertainty into any programme. If the deferment clause is not stated to apply, there is a serious breach of contract as described under MW, MWD below.

60
Letter from architect to contractor, if important drawings not available

Dear

[*insert appropriate heading*]

Thank you for your letter of [*insert date*].

Will you let me have full evidence in support of your assertion as soon as possible.

It is not usual, as you know, to supply every single detail at the commencement of the contract. However, if you will let me have precise information regarding the drawings and schedules you need immediately, including why you need them at this stage, I will ensure that any necessary drawings are sent to you.

Yours faithfully

IC, ICD

The position under these contracts is broadly similar. The clauses under which you should grant an extension of time and under which the contractor may make application for reimbursement of loss and/or expense are 2.20.3 and 4.17.1 respectively. If the deferment clause (2.5) is not stated to apply, there is a serious breach of contract as described under MW, MWD below.

MW, MWD

There is no provision for deferment under these forms of contract and failure to give possession is very serious. It is a serious breach and the contractor can terminate its employment under clause 6.8.2.2 or, under certain circumstances, treat it as repudiation at common law, bring the contract to an end and recover substantial damages. You must do two things:

- Through the employer, ensure possession of the entire site as soon as possible
- Try to get the contractor to agree in writing to put back the commencement and completion dates by the necessary amount. This amounts to varying the contract terms, which requires the employer's authority. If the contractor agrees, you should ensure that both parties amend, and initial, the printed conditions accordingly. The contractor may also wish to claim some damages but that is usually preferable to termination. Each case must be judged on its merits (**61**). It will be unusual for a contractor to refuse to agree new dates, if some recompense for the delayed start is promised

Immediately inform the employer of the situation by telephone. If the revised date for possession is not agreed by the contractor, the employer will have to face the consequences.

K6   Meetings: standing of minutes as a record (62), (63)

Minutes are often referred to by the contractor or architect in claims for extension of time or loss and/or expense. Provided that there is a proper record at each meeting that the minutes of the previous meeting are agreed by all parties, the minutes will stand as a true record of the matters contained therein. Lack of recorded agreement reduces their standing and value considerably to that of a mere note produced by one side only. This is not to say they have no value. They may well be of crucial importance, particularly if there is no evidence to the contrary. Where the contract requires the issue of certificates of any kind, written notices or instructions, you should not attempt to issue them as part of the minutes. Their standing would be, at best, doubtful.

You should make it clear that you will chair your contract meetings and produce the minutes. It will enable you to ensure that all items discussed are

61
Letter from architect to contractor, if possession not given on due date and no deferment provision

Dear

[*insert appropriate heading*]

I have been informed by my client that possession of the site/whole site [*delete as appropriate*] will not be possible on the due date.

However, I am assured that possession will be given on [*insert date*]. I have suggested that both the date for commencement[1] and the date for completion should be set back by [*insert number of days related to delay in possession*] days and that the contract should be amended accordingly. If you agree with this course of action, I should be pleased if you would let me know as soon as possible.

Yours faithfully

Copy: Employer

[[1] *Substitute 'possession' when using SBC or IC or ICD.*]

recorded to your satisfaction. If the contractor chairs the meeting or sends you minutes of other meetings which it has held, you must check them carefully for errors and implications. Write immediately if there is anything with which you disagree (**62**). Do not wait until the next meeting. If the contractor sends you its own version of your meeting, you should return it with an appropriate response (**63**).

K7   Master programme: alleged approval by architect (64), (65), (66)

The 1980 Standard Form of Contract was the first JCT contract to make any reference to the contractor's master programme. Its successor, the Standard Building Contract 2005 (SBC), contains a similar provision in clause 2.9.1.2. It requires the contractor to supply two copies to the architect and update it within fourteen days of any revision of the completion date caused by the architect giving an extension of time. In doing so, it simply states in the printed conditions what has long been present in most contracts through an appropriate clause in the bills of quantities, schedule of work or specification. It is possible to delete the provision, of course, although this is not something which any architect should seriously consider. Although the contract conditions do not state the form the programme should take, it is usual for the architect to specify the type of programme required in the bills of quantities, schedules of work or specification, e.g. bar chart, network analysis, precedence diagram etc.

   The provision of a programme is particularly important for the purpose of:

- Accurately monitoring the contractor's actual compared to its proposed progress
- Estimating a fair and reasonable extension of time
- Deciding upon the validity of a claim for prolongation costs

   For these purposes, a precedence diagram or network analysis is invaluable.

   Depending upon the precise facts, the status of the contractor's programme may not be absolutely clear. Provided it is not signed and bound in with the contract documents nor accepted as part of the contractor's tender, it is not a contract document. Therefore, it is not something with which all parties must comply. Sometimes the bills of quantities unwisely call for you to approve the contractor's programme. It is not clear whether your approval of the programme has any real significance. If it can be shown that you have approved the programme it may be evidence that you considered the time periods and, perhaps, dates for receipt of drawings to be reasonable, but it does not make you liable for the information on the programme. Even with your approval, the programme remains a record of the contractor's intentions, not yours. Approval of the programme may not be significant but it is best not to put it to the test.

62
Letter from architect to contractor regarding items in minutes of meeting

Dear

[*insert appropriate heading*]

I have examined the minutes of the meeting held on site on [*insert date*] which I received today. I have the following comments to make:

[*insert list of comments*]

Please arrange to have these comments published at the next meeting and inserted in the appropriate place in the minutes.

Yours faithfully

Copies: To all those present at the meeting and included in the original circulation

63
Letter from architect to contractor, if contractor sends its own version of meeting

Dear

[*insert appropriate heading*]

Thank you for your letter of [*insert date*] with which you enclosed what appear to be your own notes of the meeting held on [*insert date*].

There appears to be a misunderstanding. The position is that I will chair and produce minutes for all meetings which I call in connection with this contract. If there is anything with which you disagree, it should be raised at the next meeting or by letter to me as appropriate. By now, you will have received the minutes of the above meeting. Your own notes are, therefore, returned with this letter.

Yours faithfully

It is better to require the programme to be submitted for your comment. When you receive the programme, you will certainly make some comment if it does not appear to correspond with the contract period. Do not fall into the trap of asking the contractor to change the programme but certainly ask questions about it. It is the contractor's general right to organise the construction work in any way it chooses. If you have required the programme to be submitted for your approval, it may seem reasonable that if you do not object, you approve, although the better view is that in such cases approval must be expressed and cannot be presumed by silence. In any event, you should take great care when you receive the master programme (**64**).

The contractor will often allege that the architect has approved the programme, in order perhaps to bolster its claim for an extension of time which depends upon failure to achieve some programmed dates.

IC, ICD, MW and MWD

There is no reference to a master programme in the conditions, but it is still possible to require one in the specification and in such a case the above remarks and the letter are applicable.

If you did not write this kind of letter, making your respective positions perfectly clear, the contractor may, usually at a much later date, in the process of a claim, allege your approval. There are two possible letters in reply. One, if you have never actually stated that you approved the programme, another if you have been unwise enough to indicate approval in writing (**65**), (**66**).

K8   Master programme – if contractor changes it (67)

A curious feature of the clause which requires the contractor to supply copies of the master programme is that the contractor is only required to revise the programme, or to be precise provide a copy of the revision to the architect, if there has been an extension of time. Therefore, no matter how much a programme changes or how inapplicable it becomes as a result of the contractor's own inefficiencies or mistakes, the contractor cannot be required to provide a new copy. Indeed, the contractor cannot be required to comply with the programme, because it is not a contract document. It is merely a contractual document, i.e., one that has been produced as a result of a contractual requirement. A prudent architect will have ensured that the entry in the bill of quantities or specification preliminaries which deals with the programme will include a requirement for the contractor to issue a revised copy of the programme on the reasonable request of the architect.

The situation can become difficult, however, if such a requirement has not been included and the architect is left with only the bare contract clause on which to rely. If you believe it to be essential to see a revised programme, try a letter.

64
Letter from architect to contractor, referring to the master programme

Dear

[*insert appropriate heading*]

Thank you for your letter of [*insert date*] with which you enclosed two copies of your master programme.

I have the following points to make:

[*insert a list of all the points on which you are doubtful. It is best to write them in the form of questions, e.g. are you satisfied that you have allowed sufficient time to complete the central heating, bearing in mind the other internal works you propose to carry out at the same time?*]

I have no further comments to make at this time, but you must not take any lack of comment to indicate approval to the programme in part or in whole. The organisation and method of working and the time allocated to particular activities is your responsibility to carry out within the constraints laid down by the contract, the drawings and bills of quantities/schedules of work/specification [*delete as applicable*].

Your master programme is received as an indication of your intentions only. The use of the programme as evidence in any future consideration of extension of time or loss and/or expense is a matter for my discretion.

Yours faithfully

65
Letter from architect to contractor refuting approval, if approval not given to the master programme

Dear

[*insert appropriate heading*]

Thank you for your letter of [*insert date*] to which I will reply in detail in due course.

Before I do so, however, I must put on record that I have never given approval to your master programme in part or in whole. Indeed, it would have been quite inappropriate for me to do so because the responsibility for carrying out the work, including the method of working and time, is yours, subject only to the constraints laid down in the contract, the drawings and bills of quantities/schedules of work/specification [*delete as appropriate*].

That is not to say, of course, that I will not take your programme into consideration in arriving at my decision. It is a matter for my discretion.

Yours faithfully

66
Letter from architect to contractor qualifying approval, if approval already given to the master programme

Dear

[*insert appropriate heading*]

Thank you for your letter of [*insert date*] to which I will reply in detail in due course.

Before I do so, however, I should clarify the situation in respect of the approval to the master programme you allege was given in my letter of [*insert date*].

[*Omit the following paragraph if IC, ICD, MW or MWD used.*]

Clause 2.9.1 provides that no obligations are imposed upon the parties by the master programme beyond those imposed by the contract documents.

Approval does not remove from you the responsibility for the information set out in the programme. Approval does not make me responsible for any errors or miscalculations in your programme. Approval merely indicates that I have no objection if you wish to set about constructing the project in accordance with the sequence of work and the individual time scales you have indicated. It cannot remove your responsibility for ensuring that the work is carried out in accordance with the contract.

Yours faithfully

67
Letter from architect to contractor requesting a revised programme

Dear

[*insert appropriate heading*]

The only copy of a programme in my possession is dated [*insert date*]. It is clear from visits to site, to say nothing of your progress reports and those from the clerk of works, that there is a quite significant difference between actual progress and the programme. Although there is nothing in the contract which expressly requires you to provide me with a revised programme in such circumstances, the absence of an up-to-date programme showing your current intentions seriously hinders my ability to issue information and instructions at the appropriate time. This could affect the length of any extension of time to which you may become entitled in the future.

Therefore, I should be grateful to receive your revised programme, say within the next week.

Yours faithfully

IC, ICD, MW and MWD

The comments and letter are generally applicable to these contracts where there is a requirement for a programme in the specification.

K9 Printed conditions and bills of quantities (or specification) not in agreement (68)

Over-zealousness or lack of communication between architect and quantity surveyor can lead to contradictions occurring between the printed conditions and the bills of quantities, schedules of work or specification. The areas in which such differences can occur are limitless, but a simple example would be where the bills of quantities attempt to extend the period for making payment on a certificate beyond the limits clearly defined by the conditions.

Sometimes the contractor seeks to rely on the provisions in the bills of quantities or specification, but more often it is the employer, through his representative, the architect, who wants to rely on them.

Clause 1.3 of the conditions states: 'nothing contained in the Contract Bills or the CPD Documents shall override or modify the Agreement or these Conditions'. (Clauses 1.3 of IC and ICD and 1.2 of MW and MWD are to much the same effect although variously referring to contract drawings, specifications, schedules, schedules of work or employer's requirements.)

Although the general law is that type (or handwriting) prevails over print, it is now established that clause 1.3 is effective to reverse that rule so far as SBC and similar contracts are concerned. Note that the clause only comes into effect if the bills of quantities etc., seek to 'override or modify' so that the bills of quantities etc., can contain instructions for the work to be done in a particular sequence or introduce other matters which will be binding provided they do not attempt to override or modify what is in the printed form.

Assuming that you have received a challenge from the contractor on the grounds that the conditions say something different from what is contained in the bills of quantities (or specification) you must concede, provided that the contractor is correct of course and that an overriding or modification is involved and not simply an extension or clarification (**68**).

K10 Work not in accordance with comments on the submitted documents (69)

There may be certain parts of the building, such as perhaps the heating system, which you have identified in the recitals and in the employer's requirements as 'the Contractor's Designed Portion'. The contractor must provide contractor's proposals showing how it intends to satisfy the employer's requirements and an analysis of the relevant portion of the contract sum. Clause 2.9.3 and schedule 1

68
Letter from architect to contractor referring to conflict between conditions and bills of quantities (or specification)

Dear

[*insert appropriate heading*]

Thank you for your letter of [*insert date*].

The point you raise is valid.

[*That is all you need to say; the less said the better. Depending upon the point at issue, however, you may be able to add a paragraph attacking the situation from another angle such as:*]

I would, however, draw your attention to clause [*insert clause number*] which deals with the matter in dispute.

Yours faithfully

set out the procedure governing the submission of design documents by the contractor. The contractor must provide you with two copies of such design documents as are reasonably necessary to explain and amplify the contractor's proposals and any levels and setting out information. The contractor must not do any work contained in the documents until it has complied with the procedure. There is a very simple and generally understood system by which you are to grade the submissions A, B or C.

There is seldom any real confusion or difficulty in regard to those submissions which you return marked 'A' (which the contractor may proceed to construct without change) or those which you have marked 'C' (which must be resubmitted taking your comments into account). Inevitably, the contractor may sometimes proceed to construct work shown in a document which you have marked 'B' without incorporating the changes. These are documents on which you have marked comments and which the contractor is obliged to incorporate in the work, but it can proceed provided it promptly sends a copy of the amended documents to you. The contractor may be slow to send you the revised documents or you may never receive them, since their receipt is not a prerequisite before construction proceeds. The first time you know that something is wrong may well be when you notice it on site. In such a case, you should write to the contractor immediately (**69**).

IC, ICD and MW, MWD

'Contractor's Designed Portion' work is dealt with in the ICD and MWD versions of IC and MW respectively. ICD deals with the supply of information in clause 2.10.3, but there is no express provision for a submission procedure. However, the clause makes clear that a submission procedure may be included in the contract documents. MWD deals with information in clause 2.1.5. Again, there is no submission procedure, but clause 2.1.6 requires the contractor to wait seven days before commencing work shown on any submitted documents. Letter **69** is generally applicable.

K11   Discrepancy between bills of quantities, schedules of work, specification, architect's instructions, CDP documents or statutory requirements and contract documents, not found by the contractor (70)

It is well established that your obligation is to provide the contractor with correct information. The contractor has no obligation to check the drawings for discrepancies. Naturally, if it is carrying out its job properly, it should find discrepancies as it plans its work, but if they are not discovered until they have been constructed, it seems that you are in a very tough position.

The contractor also has to use proper skill and care in carrying out the Works, of course, and if you suspect that the real reason for failure to detect the

69
Letter from architect to contractor, if work not in accordance with submitted CDP drawings

Dear

[*insert appropriate heading*]

On [*insert date*], you submitted [*identify the documents*] showing [*describe the subject of the submission*]. You will recall that I returned them with my comments [*when using SBC add: 'marked "B"'*] on [*insert date*].

During my visit to site today I noticed that you were constructing the work without taking my comments into account. This is not in accordance with the contract and amounts to a breach of contract on your part. Take this as notice that I expect you immediately to alter the work on site to conform to my comments and by close of business on [*insert date*] I must have received the documents amended in accordance with my comments. Failure to comply will result in an instruction being issued in accordance with clause 3.181[1] to remove from site the work not in accordance with the contract.

Yours faithfully

[*[1] Substitute '3.16.1' when using IC or ICD and '3.4' when using MW or MWD.*]

70
Letter from architect to contractor, if discrepancy not discovered before construction

Dear

[*insert appropriate heading*]

I refer to [*insert a description of the problem*].

I find it difficult to understand how any contractor, let alone one of your undoubted experience, could have proceeded with the construction of [*briefly describe*]. There is, admittedly, a discrepancy between . . . and [*insert names of documents*], but it is just the kind of inconsistency which you could have been expected to discover as you were planning to carry out the work.

Before I can feel justified in seeking authorisation for further expenditure in this matter, I should be pleased if you would let me have a brief report setting down exactly how it was possible for you to reach this stage without finding the discrepancy. In the report, you should make reference to the precise documents you consulted before ordering and construction stages.

Yours faithfully

Copy: Quantity surveyor

discrepancy is carelessness or even malice, you should make the appropriate inquiries before you issue any instructions.

K12   Certification, if claim not yet ascertained (71), (72), (73)

Clause 4.4 of the conditions of contract stipulates that if the contract sum is to be adjusted by an amount, then as soon as the amount is ascertained in whole or in part, it should be taken into account in the computation of the next interim certificate following the ascertainment.

Problems tend to arise because, understandably, the contractor will press for the implementation of clause 4.4 at the earliest possible moment, sometimes even going so far as to accuse you of being in breach of your duty under the contract. Apart from extra work, which is relatively easy to ascertain, the commonest areas for which the contractor seeks extra payment are claims for loss and/or expense and fluctuations. Claims for loss and/or expense will be dealt with later but the principle for your reply should be the same in each case:

- Where the contractor has not provided such details as are reasonably necessary for ascertainment to take place (**71**)
- Where the contractor has provided all details necessary, but ascertainment has not taken place (**72**), (**73**).

Without doubt, the contractor will write or telephone you, demanding to know what further information you could possibly require. The best thing is to arrange for the quantity surveyor to write directly to the contractor, giving a list of the information needed (**72**).

IC, ICD

Clause 5 provides for variations and provisional sums, and clauses 4.7 and 4.9 allow for adjustment of the certificates. Clauses 4.17 and 4.18 provide for the ascertainment of loss and/or expense.

MW, MWD

Clauses 3.6 and 3.7 provide for variations and provisional sums, and clauses 4.3 and 4.5 allow for adjustment of the certificates. Letter **73** is applicable.

Provision is made for the appointment of a quantity surveyor although not referred to in the conditions. It is assumed that no quantity surveyor has been appointed and, therefore, letter **72** is not applicable.

71
Letter from architect to contractor about ascertainment, if necessary details not provided

This letter is not usually suitable for use with MW or MWD

Dear

[*insert appropriate heading*]

Thank you for your letter of [*insert date*].

I can understand your anxiety to receive all monies due to you as soon as possible. In order to achieve that end, you have a duty to provide all information reasonably necessary for the ascertainment to be carried out. The information required was requested in the quantity surveyor's letter dated [*insert date*]. It has not yet been provided. As soon as it is received, the ascertainment will be carried out as quickly as practicable and the monies, if any, due will be included in the next certificate following such ascertainment.

Yours faithfully

Copy: Quantity surveyor

72
Letter from architect asking the quantity surveyor to write to the contractor regarding ascertainment

This letter is not usually suitable for use with MW or MWD

Dear

[*insert appropriate heading*]

I have received a telephone call from the main contractor/I have received a letter from the main contractor [*use the appropriate phrase*] dated [*insert date*], a copy of which is enclosed.

The contractor is obviously anxious to get any money to which it may be entitled as soon as possible. It considers that it has sent all the information required for ascertainment.

Will you write to the contractor please, and provide a list of everything still required before the process of ascertainment can proceed?

Naturally, I do not expect you to do any calculations until you are fully satisfied that you have all the information you need.

Yours faithfully

73
Letter from architect to contractor, when information has been provided but ascertainment has not taken place

Dear

[*insert appropriate heading*]

Thank you for your letter of [*insert date*].

You submitted/The quantity surveyor informs me that you submitted [*use appropriate phrase*] the last items of information necessary for the ascertainment on [*insert date*]. <u>The quantity surveyor is proceeding with the</u>[1] checking and calculations as quickly as possible. It is conceivable that, in the course of ascertainment, there may be one or two points which require clarification. <u>In order to save as much time as possible, I am asking the quantity surveyor to write directly to you on such items.</u>[2]

[*Add only if the contractor alleges that you are in breach:*]

I reject your suggestion that <u>either the quantity surveyor or myself is</u>[3] in breach. <u>We are carrying out our</u>[4] duties strictly in accordance with the contract and with complete fairness to you and the employer.

Yours faithfully

Copy: Quantity surveyor

[[1] *Substitute 'I am proceeding with my' when using MW or MWD.*
[2] *Omit underlined words when using MW or MWD.*
[3] *Substitute 'I am' when using MW or MWD.*
[4] *Substitute 'I am carrying out my' when using MW or MWD.*]

K13   Certification: certificate not received by the employer (74)

Clause 1.9 provides that except where specifically so provided, any certificate to be issued by the architect shall be issued to the employer with a duplicate copy immediately to the contractor.

Clause 4.13.1 provides that the final date for payment to the contractor is fourteen days from the date of issue of each interim certificate. It is common practice for the fourteen-day period to be amended to twenty-one or even twenty-eight days. Clause 1.9 applies to any certificate for any purpose which the architect may issue, but difficulties most often occur with financial certificates, for obvious reasons.

It is obviously important that the employer receives the certificate at the earliest possible moment, particularly so in the case of a local authority or some other large public body where the issue of cheques follows a special procedure. You can adopt one of a number of measures to ensure that there are no hiccups at this vital stage (the contractor can suspend performance of all its obligations or even commence steps to terminate its employment under the contract if it is not paid on time – clauses 4.14 and 8.9.1.1 respectively):

- Take the certificate to the employer by hand on the day of issue
- Send the certificate by special or recorded delivery
- Telephone the employer on the day of issue, notifying the sums involved and send the certificate by first class post

Delivery by hand is the most satisfactory, if the distance is not too great, because it combines certainty with minimum delay. Remember to have a form of receipt ready for the employer to sign and date for your records. The problem is that there will be many things that you do which are of great importance, of which the issue of the certificate is but one. It is totally impractical to take everything to everybody by hand unless your organisation is large enough to employ a special messenger. It is all too easy to slip into the habit of sending certificates by first class post and assuming that they will arrive on the employer's desk the following day. Despite what is said about postal services, this method will work quite satisfactorily in the vast majority of cases. But there may be a mistake on the envelope or, for some other reason, the employer may not receive the certificate. The first intimation you are likely to receive is when the employer telephones you to say that a notice has been received from the contractor giving seven or fourteen days to pay on threat of suspension or termination of employment respectively. What is your position and what should you do?

- You have already issued the certificate at the proper time (events show that the contractor must have received a copy) so you have fulfilled your duty, but in the circumstances the employer is unlikely to be impressed

● Send a duplicate copy to the employer by hand – whatever the cost – together with a letter (**74**)

IC, ICD

The scheme of certificates is much the same as SBC, although simpler. Clause 1.9 provides that they are to be issued to the employer with a copy to the contractor. Clause 4.8.1 stipulates that payment is to be made within fourteen days of the date of issue. The other remarks and letter **74** are applicable to this form also.

MW, MWD

Although it is not entirely clear to whom the certificates should be issued, commonsense suggests that they should be issued to the employer, because it is the employer's duty to pay within fourteen days of the date of the certificate. Naturally, at the same time, you will issue a copy to the contractor. Clauses 4.3 and 4.5 make it clear that the final date for payment is within fourteen days of the date of issue of the certificate. The obligation of the employer to pay within a particular period is established and, therefore, the bulk of the general remarks in this section, except those specifically referring to clause numbers of the standard form, apply. Letter **74** is appropriate also. Fortunately, provided the employer acts promptly, ill effects can be avoided.

K14   Certification: contractor threatening to suspend, because the architect has undercertified (75)

Clause 4.14, in conformity with the Housing Grants, Construction and Regeneration Act 1996, entitles the contractor to give seven days' written notice of intention to suspend performance of its obligations if the employer, without serving a withholding notice under clause, fails to pay the amount in any certificate. A contractor often confuses the employer's failure to pay with the architect's failure to certify what the contractor believes is the proper amount. The employer's obligation to pay does not start until the architect has issued a certificate. The employer has no obligation to pay money which has not been certified. If, despite the absence of a certificate, the contractor writes demanding payment from the employer or even threatens adjudication, try a letter of explanation.

IC, ICD and MW, MWD

The position is the same under these contracts.

74
Letter from architect to employer, if certificate has not arrived on time

Dear

[*insert appropriate heading*]

I refer to your telephone call today.

A copy of certificate number [*insert number*] is enclosed. It is essential that you take whatever steps are necessary to get a cheque for the full amount to the contractor immediately. It is inadvisable to assume that you have a full seven[1] days to pay because, technically, the certificate is not discharged until your cheque has been cleared through the bank. I suggest that you arrange to have the cheque delivered by hand, but be sure to obtain a signed and dated receipt.

If you allow the contractor to terminate its employment/suspend performance of its obligations [*delete as appropriate*] the consequences will be extensive extra cost and considerable delay to the project.

I issued the certificate on [*insert date*]. Why you have not received it is not known and is of academic interest only in the present circumstances. This is the first time that this problem has occurred but, to avoid a repetition in the future, all certificates will be sent to you by special delivery and I will arrange to telephone you within two days of the date of issue to check that you have received them.

Yours faithfully

[[1] *Substitute 'fourteen' if the contractor is threatening termination under SBC, IC or ICD.*]

75
Letter from architect to contractor, if seeking payment without a certificate

Dear

[*insert appropriate heading*]

Thank you for your letter dated [*insert date*] alleging that the employer is somehow in default for failing to pay you money not yet certified.

Your argument is misconceived. Under the contract, the employer has an obligation to pay only money which has been properly certified and for which the employer does not wish to serve a withholding notice.

[*If the contractor is threatening adjudication, add:*]

Consequently, if you persist in seeking adjudication on this point, you will be doomed to failure.

Yours faithfully

K15   Certification: if there is a serious defect less than five days before the final date for payment (76)

A nightmare scenario is where a serious defect comes to light just after the deadline for the issue of a withholding notice has passed. Although this does not happen on a regular basis, anecdotal evidence suggests that it happens more often than one might think. Contract clause 4.13.4 is clear about the time schedule. If the final date for payment is closer than five days it seems that the full amount certified or stated in a proposal for payment under clause 4.13.3 must be paid. Everything hinges upon the amount due as indicated in clause 4.13.5. Where the amount due is to be the amount in an architect's certificate, it is doubtful that payment can be avoided. However, try a letter.

IC, ICD and MW, MWD

The position is identical under these contracts. The clause numbers, of course, are different. Letter **76** is applicable.

K16   Instruction: contractor's refusal to carry out forthwith (77), (78), (79), (80), (81), (Flowchart 1)

Clause 3.10 deals with the contractor's obligation to comply forthwith with all instructions you issue in respect of matters on which you are expressly empowered by the conditions to issue instructions. There are two exceptions. Firstly variations within the meaning of clause 5.1.2, when the contractor need not comply to the extent that it makes reasonable objection to the architect in writing. Whether the objection is reasonable is something to be decided, first by the architect and ultimately, if there is a dispute, by an adjudicator or an arbitrator. You would be advised to consider any objection by the contractor very carefully before deciding that it is not reasonable. Secondly, it is thought that on the wording of clause 3.13, if the contractor, after requesting you to specify the clause empowering the instruction, decides to seek dispute resolution, it has the right to await the outcome of the procedure before complying.

If the contractor receives a perfectly straightforward instruction and, far from carrying it out forthwith, appears to be taking no action whatever, you can send a notice in accordance with clause 3.11 (**77**).

If the contractor continues to default, you should record the fact (**78**).

Employer: accepts new quotation

You can proceed to arrange for the work to be done by the others. If you decide to take this action, and there may not be any alternative, it is advisable to obtain three quotations for carrying out the work if the work in question lends itself to this method of approach. The reason is because, in recovering costs from the

76
Letter from architect to contractor, if a serious defect has been discovered

Dear

[*insert appropriate heading*]

Thank you for your letter dated [*insert date*] alleging that the employer is in default for failing to pay the amount stated on certificate dated [*insert date*].

Clause 4.16.1.1 makes clear that the amount to be included in an interim certificate is the value of work properly executed. I have already informed you that serious defects, which amount to a breach or breaches of contract on your part, have just been discovered in the work. Therefore, the work for which a value has been included in this certificate was not properly executed. In these circumstances, the employer is entitled to exercise an abatement of the certified amount and you should receive such notification directly from the employer.

Yours faithfully

77
Letter from architect to contractor, giving notice requiring compliance with an instruction

SPECIAL/RECORDED DELIVERY [*as appropriate*]

Dear

[*insert appropriate heading*]

Take this as notice under clause $4.1.2^1$ of the conditions of contract that I require you to comply with my instruction number [*insert number*] dated [*insert date*], a further copy of which is enclosed.

If within seven days of receipt of this notice you have not complied, the employer may employ and pay other persons to execute any work whatsoever which may be necessary to give effect to the instruction. All costs incurred in connection with such employment will be deducted from money due or to become due to you under the contract or will be recovered from you as a debt.

Yours faithfully

Copies: Employer
          Quantity surveyor

[^{1} *Substitute '3.5.1' when using IC or ICD and '3.5' when using MW or MWD.*]

78
Letter from architect to contractor, if contractor fails to comply within seven days (date at least seven days from previous notice)

SPECIAL/RECORDED DELIVERY [*as appropriate*]

Dear

[*insert appropriate heading*]

I refer to the notice issued to you on [*insert date*] in accordance with clause 4.1.2[1] referring to my instruction number [*insert number*] dated [*insert date*].

I confirm that I have inspected the Works this morning and you have not complied with my instruction.

The employer is taking immediate steps to employ others to carry out the work. All costs in connection with such employment will be deducted from the contract sum.

Yours faithfully

Copies: Employer
          Quantity surveyor

[[1] *Substitute '3.5.1' when using IC or ICD and '3.5' when using MW or MWD.*]

contractor, you ought to be able to show that the employer has made reasonable efforts to have the work done at the lowest practicable price. In the case of an instruction for additional work, you will be seeking to recover costs which will be the difference between the actual cost and the contractor's bill rates, plus incidental costs which can include your additional fees. You will have to use your discretion as to whether the time scale of the work allows you to seek quotations.

Complications occur if the contractor carries out the instruction at the thirteenth hour, after the employer has already accepted a quotation from another firm (**79**).

Note that communications to the contractor must deal precisely with four points:

- Relevant dates
- Relevant clauses of the conditions
- Failure by contractor
- Financial consequences to the contractor

Contractor: seeks to agree new date

After receipt of your notice to comply in accordance with clause 3.11, it is not unusual for the contractor to claim that your instruction has not been carried out forthwith, because it does not fit in with the work programme. The contractor may, however, promise to carry out the work by a specific date. You must consider all aspects of the contract carefully before agreeing to this proposal, being careful to preserve the employer's rights (**80**). In most cases you will probably reject these suggestions (**81**).

It is never easy to decide to employ others on the contractor's work. It sours relationships. Generally, it is less damaging when the project is almost complete rather than in the initial stages.

IC, ICD

Architect's instructions are dealt with by clauses 3.8, 3.9 and 3.10. It is similar to SBC except that there is no provision for confirming oral instructions. Letters **77** to **81** inclusive, **Flowchart 1** and the other general remarks in this section are applicable.

MW, MWD

Clauses 3.4 and 3.5 relate to architect's instructions. They are very brief and state that the architect may issue written instructions 'which the contractor shall forthwith comply with'. There is no provision for the contractor to object (except of course by adjudication or arbitration), but there is provision for a seven days compliance notice in similar terms to that of the standard form. Letters **77** to **81**

79
Letter from architect to contractor, if the contractor carries out instructions after another firm's quotation is accepted

Dear

[*insert appropriate heading*]

You were instructed to carry out the work contained in my instruction number [*insert number*] dated [*insert date*]. Clause 3.10[1] requires you to comply with instructions forthwith. This you failed to do.

In accordance with clause 3.11[2], I sent you a notice dated [*insert date*] requiring you to comply with my instruction within seven days. On [*insert date*] I notified you that you were in breach of your obligations under the contract and the work would be carried out by others. Subsequently, on [*insert date*], you carried out the instruction.

The employer has been subject to costs in connection with the employment of others and, in accordance with clause 3.11[3], those costs will be deducted from the contract sum.

Yours faithfully

Copies: Employer
          Quantity surveyor

[[1] *Substitute '3.5.1' when using IC or ICD and '3.4' when using MW or MWD.*
[2] *Substitute '3.9' when using IC or ICD and '3.5' when using MW or MWD.*
[3] *Substitute '3.9' when using IC or ICD and '3.5' when using MW or MWD.*]

80
Letter from architect to contractor, agreeing to a later date for carrying out instructions

Dear

[*insert appropriate heading*]

Thank you for your letter of [*insert date*].

I note that you propose to complete the work detailed in my instruction number [*insert number*] dated [*insert date*] on [*insert date*].

After careful consideration, I am prepared to agree to your proposal on the understanding that the employer does not waive any rights and remedies under the contract. This means that if you default in completing the work on [*insert contractor's proposed date*] the notice sent to you on [*insert date*] will have expired and, without further notice, the employer will employ others to carry out the work.

Yours faithfully

Copies: Employer
          Quantity surveyor

81
Letter from architect to contractor, not agreeing to a later date for carrying out instructions

Dear

[*insert appropriate heading*]

Thank you for your letter of [*insert date*].

Having carefully considered your proposals to complete the work detailed in my instruction number [*insert number*] dated [*insert date*], I regret that I cannot agree.

The notice sent to you on [*insert date*] will shortly expire and you are strongly urged to put the work in hand before that date to avoid the employer taking action to employ others to do the work at considerable extra cost to yourself.

[*If the notice has already expired by the time you write this letter, omit the last paragraph and substitute the three paragraphs of letter* **78**.]

Yours faithfully

Copies: Employer
           Quantity surveyor

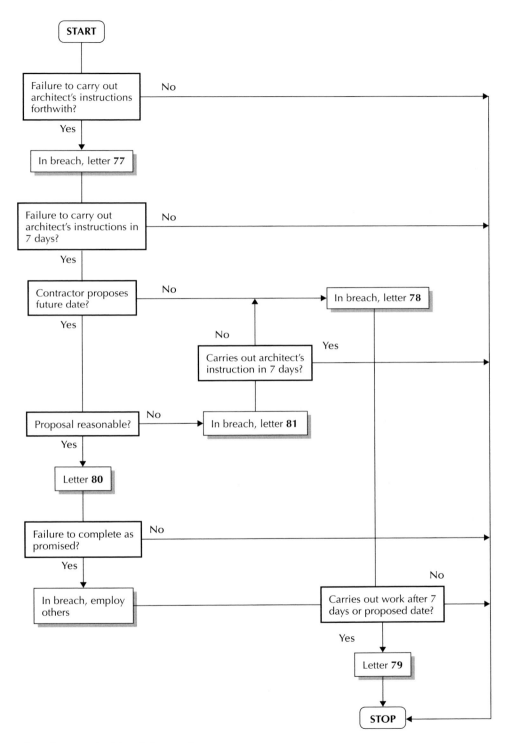

Flowchart 1   Architect's instructions.

inclusive are applicable, as are the other general remarks in this section. **Flowchart 1** is also appropriate.

K17   Instructions: by building control officer (82), (83), (84), (Flowchart 2)

The building control officer will usually inspect the Works in progress as part of normal duties. Although not empowered to do so, if anything is found which is not in accordance with the Building Regulations, the building control officer will very often give oral instructions to the person-in-charge on site to correct the problem. The contractor may carry out the instruction and present the result to you as a *fait accompli*, demanding extra payment. You should adopt a procedure best illustrated by **Flowchart 2**. (The clause numbers on the flowchart are only applicable to the standard form.)

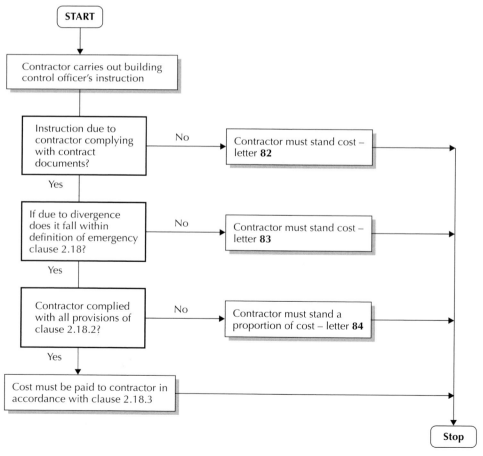

Flowchart 2   Building control officer's instructions.

IC, ICD

Statutory obligations are covered by clauses 2.1 and 2.15. Emergency compliance is covered by clause 2.16. **Flowchart 2** and letters **82** to **84** are applicable with the amendments indicated.

MW, MWD

Clauses 2.1.1 and 2.5 (2.6 in ICD) deal with statutory obligations. There is no procedure for emergencies. The contractor, however, may claim an emergency. Letters **82** to **84** inclusive are applicable with the amendments indicated. **Flowchart 2** relates to the standard form but it may be used as a general guide to the procedure you can adopt to decide whether there was an emergency and to what extent the contractor must bear the costs.

A similar procedure would be suitable if any other statutory authority was concerned.

K18   Setting out: architect requested to check (85), (86), (87), (88), (Instruction 1)

Clause 2.10 requires you to determine any levels required for the execution of the Works and to supply accurately dimensioned drawings so that the contractor can set out the Works.

It is common for the contractor to request the architect to check the setting out. The architect normally complies and will often confirm the accuracy. It is dangerous to do that, because it tends to relieve the contractor of responsibility for errors. It is, of course, quite sensible for you to carry out any dimensional checks on site you wish in order to fulfil your obligations to your client. Be quite clear, however, that you are carrying out your own duties and not those of the contractor (**85**).

If you do visit the site and check the setting out for your own peace of mind, it is not unusual for you to receive a letter from the contractor recording your visit and confirming that you have found its setting out to be correct (**86**).

The contractor is responsible for correcting errors in its own setting out at no cost to the employer. It may be convenient, perhaps because the error is not great or because time is short, to instruct the contractor not to amend erroneous setting out. You must obtain the employer's consent first. An appropriate deduction may be made from the contract sum. The precise method of arriving at the figure is not set out in the contract. It cannot be the cost of getting others to correct the setting out. In certain circumstances, it may be what it would have cost the contractor to correct the setting out. If the employer is very little or not at all inconvenienced by the error, an appropriate deduction may be nothing at all or a relatively nominal sum. This provision does not give the employer the opportunity to make an unexpected profit. The quantity surveyor is to do the calculation (clause 4.16.3.1) and it is reasonable for you to inform the contractor of the

82
Letter from architect to contractor, if contractor complies with building control officer's instruction to correct its own error

Dear

[*insert appropriate heading*]

Thank you for your letter of [*insert date*].

I cannot consider your claim for additional costs in complying with the instructions of the building control officer because the work you corrected was not in accordance with the contract.

Yours faithfully

Copy: Quantity surveyor

83
Letter from architect to contractor, if contractor complies with building control officer's instruction to correct error due to divergence between statutory requirements and contract documents, not constituting an emergency

Dear

[*insert appropriate heading*]

I cannot consider your claim for additional costs, submitted on [*insert date*], in complying with the instructions of the building control officer for the following reasons:

1. Although the defect was allegedly due to a divergence between the contract documents and statutory requirements,
    (a) the situation did not fall into the category of an emergency <u>envisaged by clause 2.18</u>[1]
    (b) it fell under clause 2.17[2] and you failed to give me the required written notice specifying the divergence; therefore
2. I had no opportunity to issue appropriate instructions, and
3. Your action was and remains your responsibility and your cost.

Yours faithfully

Copy: Quantity surveyor

[[1] *Substitute '2.16' when using IC or ICD. Omit underlined part when using MW or MWD.*
[2] *Substitute '2.15' when using IC or ICD, '2.5' when using MW and '2.6' when using MWD.*]

84
Letter from architect to contractor, if the contractor has not complied with all the provisions of clause 2.1.8 (or 2.16 when using IC)

Dear

[*insert appropriate heading*]

Thank you for your letter of [*insert date*].

In carrying out the work instructed by the building control officer I accept that the situation was an emergency <u>envisaged by clause 2.18</u>.[1]

However, you did not [*omit one of the following phrases as appropriate*] supply limited materials and execute limited work <u>in accordance with clause 2.18.1</u>[2]/forthwith inform me of the emergency and the steps you were taking <u>as required by clause 2.18.2</u>.[3]

In the circumstances, the claim you are making for additional cost will be allowed subject to a deduction for unnecessary expense incurred by the employer due to your default(s).

Yours faithfully

Copy: Quantity surveyor

[*[1] Substitute '2.16' when using IC or ICD. Omit underlined part when using MW or MWD.*
[2] Substitute '2.16.1' when using IC or ICD. Omit underlined part when using MW or MWD.
[3] Substitute '2.16.2' when using IC or ICD. Omit underlined part when using MW or MWD.]

Architect's instruction 1: not to amend error in setting out

Not suitable for use with MW or MWD

Refer to the attached drawing number [*insert number*]. An error in setting out is apparent in the position marked A. The approximate line of the inaccurate setting out of this portion of the work is indicated on the drawing by the red line superimposed over the printed information. With the consent of the employer in accordance with clause 2.10[1] I instruct you not to amend such inaccurate setting out. An appropriate deduction will be made from the contract sum.

Copies: Employer
          Quantity surveyor
          Clerk of works

[[1] *Substitute '2.9' when using IC or ICD.*]

85
Letter from architect to contractor, replying to request to check setting out

Dear

[*insert appropriate heading*]

Thank you for your letter of [*insert date*].

The setting out of the Works on site is your responsibility under the contract. I am of the opinion that you have been provided with all necessary levels, dimensions and such information as to enable you to do so. Any inspection I may decide to carry out will not remove your obligations, neither will any lack of comment on my part imply approval of your setting out.

Yours faithfully

86
Letter from architect to contractor, replying to confirmation that setting out is correct

Dear Sir

[*insert appropriate heading*]

Thank you for your letter of [*insert date*].

The setting out of the Works on site is your responsibility <u>in accordance with clause 2.10[1] of the conditions of contract</u>. Any inspection which I make, including the taking of dimensions as I deem appropriate, does not relieve you of your responsibilities in any way.

I have not confirmed and do not confirm that your setting out is correct. Any lack of comment from me is not to be taken, in this or any other matter, to be a sign of approval.

Yours faithfully

[[1] *Substitute '2.9' when using IC or ICD. Omit underlined part when using MW or MWD.*]

amount to be deducted as soon as possible (**87**). What if the contractor replies, saying the deduction is outrageous and it will correct the setting out instead? (**88**).

IC, ICD

Setting out is covered by clause 2.9.

MW, MWD

There is no specific mention of setting out, but it is a necessary implication that you will supply all the information and the contractor has responsibility, as part of its work, for setting out. The general remarks in this section are applicable, as are letters **85** and **86** with amendments as indicated.

K19   Defective work: dealing with the problem (89), (90), (Instruction 2)

The contractor's obligations are set down very concisely in clause 2.1. Problems sometimes arise if the work, materials or goods are defective. To be 'defective' under the contract they must be, in the language of the contract, 'not in accordance with the contract'.

Defects are normally discovered by the contractor, the clerk of works or the architect. Most defects are corrected before anyone but the contractor notices. Defects found by the clerk of works and architect should be mentioned to the contractor and recorded in a clerk of works site direction. Usually that is sufficient but, if the defect is serious or the contractor shows any reluctance to attend to it immediately, it is wise to issue an instruction to cover the matter (clause 3.18.1).

The normal instruction is to remove the defective goods, materials or work from site. It is important to understand that you are not empowered by the conditions simply to require a defect occurring during the course of the work to be made good, although that seems the sensible thing to do. You do have other options. If the employer agrees, you can allow the defect to remain (unless it is part of the contractor's designed portion) and an appropriate deduction must be made when the contract sum is adjusted. The sum in this instance is usually, but not invariably, what it would cost the contractor to make good. You must consult with the contractor first and confirm the position in writing.

Removal of defective work sometimes means that it is desirable to issue a further instruction to vary other work. Insofar as the further instruction is reasonably necessary as a result of ordering removal of work (or of allowing defective work to remain), clause 3.18.3 permits the issue of such an instruction without any resultant addition to the contract sum or extension of the contract period. You must consult with the contractor first. If the contractor objects to the

87
Letter from architect to contractor, stating the amount to be deducted for errors in setting out

Not suitable for use with MW or MWD

Dear

[*insert appropriate heading*]

I refer to my instruction number [*insert number*] dated [*insert date*] regarding an error in setting out.

The amount to be deducted from the contract sum in respect of the inaccurate setting out is £[*insert amount*]. This sum represents an appropriate deduction.

Yours faithfully

88
Letter from architect to contractor, if contractor wishes to correct inaccurate setting out

Not suitable for use with MW or MWD

Dear

[*insert appropriate heading*]

Thank you for your letter of [*insert date*].

[*Then, either:*]

I note that you wish to amend the inaccurate setting out noted in my instruction number [*insert number*] dated [*insert date*]. I am pleased to consent to your request provided that [*insert any conditions you wish to impose, such as date by which the amendment must be complete, safety of adjacent work, etc.*]. Such amendment must be carried out entirely at your own cost with no damage to any other part of the Works and on the basis that you will have no claim for any loss and/or expense or extension of time in respect of such amendment. This consent and your corrective works are not to be construed as relieving you from any of your obligations under the contract nor a waiver of any of the employer's rights.

[*continued*]

---

88 continued

[*Or:*]

The instruction to which you refer was issued after having carefully considered the consequences of amending the error at this stage of the work. The employer has decided to exercise the right to consent to my instruction that the error not be amended. Your duty is to comply with my instruction forthwith. I know you are concerned regarding the amount to be deducted from the contract sum and I should be happy to discuss this aspect with you. Perhaps you would care to telephone me later in the week to arrange a meeting?

Yours faithfully

amount or kind of variation you propose to order, there is no contractual mechanism to give any weight to the objection except that the contractor may seek adjudication or whichever the parties have chosen between arbitration and legal proceedings. The crucial question for the contractor is one of money and time.

Clause 3.18.4 allows you to go further and issue instructions to open up and test part of the Works to establish to your reasonable satisfaction that there are no similar defects or, as appropriate, that the defect is no greater in extent than you have already discovered. Provided that the opening up required is reasonable, there is to be no addition to the contract sum whatever the result. The contractor may be entitled to an extension of time under clause 2.29.2.2 if the opening up showed that the materials, goods or workmanship was in accordance with the contract.

What is reasonable opening up will depend on circumstances. In order to help you to decide, a code of practice is appended to the conditions (as schedule 4) to which you must 'have due regard' before issuing your instruction. Clearly, if you can agree with the contractor the opening up required to demonstrate that the remainder of the Works contains no similar defect, that is ideal. The contractor should be anxious to satisfy you on that point. If you cannot agree, you may proceed whether the contractor agrees or not. In any subsequent dispute resolution procedure, the degree to which you took into account the matters in the code of practice would determine to what extent your instruction was reasonable 'in all the circumstances'. The code of practice is very broad in scope. If the contractor objects, you should make the position clear (**89**).

If the contractor does not carry out the instruction, you should follow the normal procedure outlined in K16.

IC, ICD

You may instruct removal of work by virtue of clause 3.16. After that, the system is different from SBC. When work or material is discovered to be not in accordance with the contract, the onus is on the contractor to give a written statement to you telling you what it proposes to do at no cost to the employer to establish that similar work is not similarly affected. You may issue your own instructions to open up or test the work if:

- The contractor has not sent you proposals within seven days of the discovery of the defect; *or*
- You are not satisfied with them; *or*
- For safety or statutory reasons you cannot wait for the proposals

The contractor has ten days after receipt of your instruction to give you written objection with reasons. If you do not withdraw your instruction or modify it to remove the objection within seven days of receipt of the objection, the matter is referred to a dispute resolution procedure to decide whether it was reasonable in all the circumstances. The contractor is not excused from complying with the

---

89
Letter from architect to contractor, if contractor objects to instruction to open up or test after non-compliance discovered

---

This letter is not suitable for use with IC, ICD, MW or MWD

Dear

[*insert appropriate heading*]

Thank you for your letter of [*insert date*] and I note that you object to carrying out the opening up/testing [*delete as appropriate*] described in my instruction number [*insert number*] dated [*insert date*] issued pursuant to clause 3.18.1 of the conditions of contract.

The instruction was issued after I had had due regard to the code of practice appended to the conditions and you should comply with the instruction forthwith.

Yours faithfully

instruction and the usual sanctions (see K16) are applicable. The extent to which the adjudicator or arbitrator finds that your instruction is not fair and reasonable will determine the amount of payment by the employer and the contractor's entitlement to an extension of time.

One of the problems with this clause is that the obligation laid on the contractor does not distinguish the severity of the defect. Thus, in theory, the contractor should give you proposals for every defect discovered no matter how small. You have no power to waive this requirement, neither would it be wise to do so, but it makes sense to achieve a clear understanding with the contractor about what it means in practice. An appropriate forum for doing this is the pre-start meeting. It is quite likely that the contractor will consider that only really major defects warrant the application of this clause and may require prompting whenever you become aware of a defect (**90**).

MW, MWD

There is no specific provision for dealing with defective work as the contract progresses but it must be implied that you can issue instructions to deal with any work not in accordance with the contract by virtue of clause 3.4. There are no specific provisions for ordering, opening up or testing after failure of work, but of course there is no reason why you should not so instruct under your general powers to instruct provided you are willing to take the risk that the work will be in accordance with the contract and an addition must be made to the contract sum. Architect's **Instruction 2** is applicable.

K20   Defective work: late instructions to remove (91), (92), (93), (94)

More often than you may care to admit, defects are discovered on site long after subsequent work has been completed (e.g. windows built in too low or too high). In such cases you will, no doubt, do everything you can to see whether the work can be made acceptable without too much additional cost to the contractor. You will try particularly hard if it comes into the category known as 'honest mistakes'. If you decide that something, other than the work or materials required by the contract, is acceptable you must obtain the employer's consent and make sure that the contractor is in the position of offering a solution at its own risk and taking full design responsibility for it, if appropriate. The trouble is that, although you may know what you would like to see done, you must beware of giving the contractor anything which can be construed as an instruction. For this purpose the device of the double letter is helpful (**91**), (**92**). The two letters are sent to the contractor at the same time.

After receiving the instruction to remove defective work, the contractor may put forward various objections. It may allege, among other things:

90
Letter from architect to contractor, after discovery of work not in accordance with the contract

This letter is not suitable for use with SBC, MW or MWD

Dear

[*insert appropriate heading*]

When visiting site today, I noted that [*describe the work or materials*] failed to be in accordance with the contract.

In accordance with clause 3.15.1 of the conditions of contract, I require you to state in writing within seven days of the date of this letter the action you will immediately take at no cost to the employer to establish that there is no similar failure in work already executed/materials or goods already supplied [*delete as appropriate*].

Yours faithfully

Architect's instruction 2: to remove defective work, materials or goods

The following work/materials/goods [*omit as appropriate*] are not in accordance with the contract and must be removed from site <u>in accordance with clause 3.18.1</u>[1].

[*List defects*]

Copies: Employer
        Quantity surveyor
        Clerk of works

[[1] *Substitute '3.16.1' when using IC or ICD. Omit underlined part when using MW or MWD.*]

91
Letter from architect to contractor (double letter 1)

Dear

[*insert appropriate heading*]

I refer to my instruction number [*insert number*] dated [*insert date*] requiring removal of defective work and to your letter of [*insert date*] asking if there is some other way of dealing with the defect.

I am always ready to consider your suggestions, but it is for you to put forward your proposals and confirm that in consideration for the employer exercising forbearance and not requiring you to remove the work, you will accept full design and construction responsibility for the results. The proposals must be at no further financial or time cost to the contract and you must accept that the employer reserves the right to change back to the original specification.

Yours faithfully

92
Letter from architect to contractor (double letter 2)

WITHOUT PREJUDICE

Dear

[*insert appropriate heading*]

With regard to the defect specified in my instruction number [*insert number*] dated [*insert date*], if you were to suggest the following, I am authorised to state that the employer would be prepared to accept it:

[*State precisely what you wish the contractor to submit to you as its suggestion, taking care to include reference to any design and construction responsibility and, if appropriate, any reimbursement of money to the employer. The contractor's offer should note that its assumption of all responsibility and reimbursement of money is in return for the employer allowing the defective work to remain.*]

Yours faithfully

- The defective work, while admittedly not quite what was required, has been in position for a considerable time and it is unreasonable to order its removal so late in the contract
- The architect and clerk of works did not make any adverse comment during many inspections
- The contractor was led to assume approval by the conduct of the architect and clerk of works
- The architect and the clerk of works deliberately waited until the last moment to condemn defective work because the employer will not be ready to occupy the Works at the contractual completion date

It is important to remember that the contractor is probably quite sincere in these accusations. From a contractor's point of view it is catastrophic to be told, for example, that the floor-to-ceiling heights are incorrect when the shell of the building is complete. Nevertheless, the position should be made quite clear to the contractor (**93**). The question really is whether the contractor has done what it undertook to do in the contract. If not, the contractor is in breach. Having said that, there are circumstances where the cost of remedying a breach will outweigh any advantage and the law will then look at what is reasonable in all the circumstances. You must be aware of that, because the law will not require a contractor to demolish a whole section of the building to achieve conformity with the contract unless there is an extremely good reason.

Suppose the contractor quotes clause 3.20 in his favour because the defect is in work which is specified to be to your 'approval' or 'satisfaction'. Your reply will depend upon precise circumstances, but letter **94** may be appropriate. It may be prudent to delete clause 3.20 so that the question does not arise.

IC, ICD and MW, MWD

The comments are generally applicable to these forms except that there is no equivalent to clause 3.20.

K21   Materials, goods and workmanship: not procurable (95), (96), (97), (98), (Instruction 3)

At some stage in almost every contract, the contractor will write informing you that some materials are not procurable. Often, something else may be suggested. The letter may mean:

- Materials not procurable at the price the contractor originally envisaged
- Materials not procurable at the appropriate time (possibly because the contractor was late in placing an order)
- Materials not procurable because they have gone out of production since the tender was submitted

93
Letter from architect to contractor, countering allegation that late instruction implies approval

Note: References to the clerk of works should be omitted when using MW or MWD if no clerk of works is employed

Dear

[*insert appropriate heading*]

In reply to your letter of [*insert date*], the position with regard to defective work or materials is quite clear. It is your responsibility under the contract to ensure that the Works are properly executed. The duty of the clerk of works is to inspect on behalf of the employer, not to carry out any of the duties of your own person-in-charge.

Neither I nor the clerk of works has any duty to inform you of defects at any particular time. Lack of comment can never be taken to indicate approval.

[*The next paragraph may be added at your discretion:*]

Without prejudice to the position already stated and the effect of the above-mentioned instructions, I recognise that you will suffer a heavy financial burden in carrying out my instruction number [*insert number*]. I am prepared to consider any alternative proposals you submit within the next week.

Yours faithfully

94
Letter from architect to contractor, if contractor quotes clause 3.20

This letter is not suitable for use with IC, ICD, MW or MWD

Dear

[*insert appropriate heading*]

Thank you for your letter of [*insert date*] in which, on the basis of clause 3.20, you object to my instruction number [*insert number*] dated [*insert date*] requiring you to remove [*list defects*] from site under the provisions of clause 3.18.1.

In the case of work falling under clause 2.3, clause 3.20 requires me to express reasons for any dissatisfaction within a reasonable time from the execution of the unsatisfactory work. What is a reasonable time cannot be considered in the abstract, but must be viewed in the light of all the circumstances. It is my opinion that I have expressed my reasons for dissatisfaction within a reasonable time in this instance. Please carry out the above noted instruction number [*insert number*] forthwith.

Yours faithfully

95
Letter from architect to contractor, if materials not procurable

Dear

[*insert appropriate heading*]

Thank you for your letter of [*insert date*].

Before I can make a decision on this matter, I should be pleased if you would supply me with the following information:

1. The date on which you placed your order.
2. Photostat copies of your order and any correspondence between the supplier and yourself.
3. Details of your attempts to obtain the materials from an alternative supplier.

Yours faithfully

96
Letter from architect to supplier, if materials not procurable

Dear

[*insert appropriate heading*]

I am informed by [*insert name of main contractor*] that you are unable to supply [*insert name or description of material*] which is specified in this contract and is required on site on [*insert date*]. I should be grateful if you would confirm the position and let me have the following information:

1.   The date on which you received the contractor's order.
2.   Any other information which might be relevant, e.g. delivery period.

Needless to say, I view the situation with concern, and your reply will obviously affect not only this contract but my specifying policy in the future.

Yours faithfully

97
Letter from architect to contractor, if it is to stand the extra costs of alternative materials

Dear

[*insert appropriate heading*]

I have now had the opportunity to consider your letters of [*insert dates of all the contractor's letters bearing on the subject*]. I have also made my own enquiries.

I am authorised to state that the employer is prepared to agree to your suggestion that the following alternative materials be used at no additional cost or delay to the contract arising either directly or indirectly from their use.

[*List the materials that the employer is prepared to accept.*]

The employer's agreement is on the clear understanding that you will accept full responsibility for the suitability and performance of the said materials and you should immediately write to the employer, through my office, giving your confirmation.

Yours faithfully

Architect's instruction 3: varying materials which are not procurable

Pursuant to clause 3.14^1 of the conditions of contract:

Omit: [*insert the materials which are not procurable, preferably stating bill of quantities or specification reference*]

Add: [*insert the materials you wish to replace them*]

[^{1} *Substitute '3.11' when using IC or ICD or '3.6' when using MW or MWD.*]

The position is as follows:

- The contractor must pay the higher price and stand the difference if that is the problem
- If the contractor was late in placing an order, it must stand the difference in cost of any reasonable alternative you allow (**97**)
- If the delivery date is just impossibly long or the materials have gone out of production, you must specify an alternative and the contract sum must be adjusted accordingly (**98**)

Before you arrive at any decision you must be certain of your facts. It is wise to write to both contractor and supplier. If you are lucky, your letters will result in the materials becoming available as if by magic. The alternative result will be that you should have sufficient information to make the decision on the merits of the case.

IC, ICD and MW, MWD

The contractor's obligations are not similarly qualified under these forms. The result is probably that if materials are not procurable, the contractor must obtain your consent to the provision of substitute materials at no additional cost to the employer. Letter **97** is applicable.

K22   Inspection: architect's duties (99) (Fig. 2)

It is essential that you carry out your duty to inspect the work with reasonable care and skill. Architects often wonder if they will be liable simply for failure to spot defective work. Obviously, the primary responsibility for executing the work correctly lies with the contractor, which should have its own system of inspection through the person in charge.

You owe no duty to the contractor to find defects, but you do owe a duty to the employer, your client. It is the extent of this duty which causes confusion. As a basic rule, you should be sure to inspect all those stages of the work which will be covered up, those with structural implications and other matters with potentially serious consequences such as damp-proofing, services, roofing, insulation and fixings of substantial elements such as stone facings.

You will never be able to inspect everything and if you miss the fact that the architraves are badly mitred or brickwork is somewhat uneven, it is unlikely to presage the end of the world.

Inspections must be approached with a plan of campaign if they are to be effective. Before the project starts on site, prepare your own programme of inspection based on the contractor's programme of work and your knowledge of the danger points. Attend site with a schedule (**Fig. 2**) on your clipboard and relevant extracts from the drawings and specification attached. Know when you

98
Letter from architect to contractor, if additional costs for alternative materials are to be allowed

Dear

[*insert appropriate heading*]

I have considered your letters of [*insert dates of all the contractor's letters bearing on the subject*]. I have also made my own enquiries.

I enclose my architect's instruction varying the materials which are not procurable to the following alternative materials.

[*List the materials*]

The variation will be valued in the usual way.

Yours faithfully

Copy: Quantity surveyor

INSPECTION SCHEDULE Project Title: Date of Possession: Date for Completion:				Inspection Date: Inspection Time:			
Order of inspection	Activity inspected	Special things to note	Result	Oral notice given: YES/NO	Written notice given: YES/NO	Re-inspection details

Fig. 2   Inspection schedule.

are going to inspect before you visit the site. Do not be deflected by the person in charge and, above all, do not simply wander onto site without clearly knowing what you want to see.

Mention any defects while you are on site and, when you get back to the office, write immediately and confirm (**99**). Importantly, you must follow up the noted defects to make sure that they have been corrected.

Do not always visit the site on the same day and do not visit only when the sun is shining!

K23   Inspection of work covered up (100), (Instruction 4)

The contract (clause 3.17) is clear that you may order the opening up of any work for inspection, but the cost of opening up and making good again

99
Letter from architect to contractor regarding defective work

Dear

[*insert appropriate heading*]

During my visit to site earlier today, I found a substantial amount of work which was not in accordance with the contract. An instruction is enclosed under clause 3.18.1[1] and I intend to re-inspect shortly.

Please make every effort to eradicate non-conforming work in the future.

Yours faithfully

Copies: Quantity surveyor
          Clerk of works

[*[1] Substitute '3.16.1' when using IC or ICD and '3.4' when using MW or MWD.*]

Architect's instruction 4: requiring work to be opened up

In accordance with clause 3.17[1] of the conditions of contract, I require you to open up [*specify the exact portion of the Works you require to be opened up*] for inspection (and testing [*if applicable*]). I intend to be present (with the clerk of works [*if applicable*]) to observe.

The work must be carried out at [*insert time*] on [*insert date*]. No opening up must begin before the time stipulated.

Failure to comply strictly with this instruction will result in you having to bear the cost of opening up and making good whatever the outcome of the inspection.

Copies: Quantity surveyor
          Clerk of works [*if applicable*]

[1 *Substitute '3.14' when using IC or ICD. Substitute '3.4' when using MW or MWD.*]

will be added to the contract sum unless the work is not in accordance with the contract.

It is vital that you arrange for any such inspection to take place on a certain day and time, and arrange to be present (with the clerk of works if there is one) to watch the opening up of the work. Otherwise, a contractor may be tempted to make good any defective work before your arrival.

IC, ICD

Opening up and inspection or testing is covered by clause 3.14 in similar terms.

MW, MWD

Clause 3.4 allows you to issue written instructions. The remarks, architect's **Instruction 4** and letter **100** in this section can be regarded as a general indication of reasonable practice. The instruction should protect you against the contractor opening up and correcting the work before you arrive.

If the work is, in fact, defective, you must immediately confirm the fact (**100**), otherwise the contractor may confirm the contrary and an argument will develop in which the one who fires the first shot may be victorious.

K24   Person-in-charge: non-notification (101)

A competent person-in-charge must be present on the site 'at all times'. The name of this person (in a contract of any size it will be the site agent or foreman) will have been notified to you at the commencement of the contract.

The contractor may change the person-in-charge without notifying you. It does happen from time to time for various reasons. You must take a very firm stand because it is essential that you know:

- That there is a person-in-charge
- The identity, so that the person-in-charge can be given instructions

IC, ICD and MW, MWD

The contractor must keep a competent person-in-charge upon the Works at all reasonable times. Generally, it will be reasonable for the person-in-charge to be on site whenever work is being carried out. It is certainly reasonable for you to know the name of the person-in-charge, and the general remarks and letter **101** in this section are applicable.

100
Letter from architect to contractor, confirming the opening up of defective work

Dear

[*insert appropriate heading*]

Together with [*name of contractor's representative*], I attended the opening up of [*specify exactly the portion of the Works opened up*] at [*insert time*] on [*insert date*]. (The clerk of works was also present [*if applicable*].)

The work was found to be not in accordance with the contract. An instruction is enclosed <u>under clause 3.18.1</u>[1] requiring removal.

When you consider the work to have been executed in accordance with the contract, <u>the clerk of works</u>[2] must be allowed to inspect before making good takes place.

<u>In accordance with clause 3.17</u>[3], the cost of opening up and making good is to be at your expense.

Yours faithfully

Copies: Quantity surveyor
          Clerk of works [*if applicable*]

[[1] *Substitute '3.14.1' when using IC or ICD. Omit when using MW or MWD.*
[2] *Substitute 'I' when using MW or MWD.*
[3] *Substitute '3.14' when using IC or ICD. Omit when using MW or MWD.*]

101
Letter from architect to contractor, requesting the name of person-in-charge

Dear

[*insert appropriate heading*]

Clause 3.2 of the conditions of contract requires you <u>to keep constantly upon the Works a competent person-in charge</u>.[1] On [*insert date*] you notified me that this person would be [*insert name*].

It has come to my attention that [*insert name*] is no longer on site[2]. If you have no person-in-charge, you are in breach of contract. I will assume that is not the case. Please notify me of the appointment and identity of the person-in-charge. Until you inform me of the identity, I am unable to issue instructions on site with any certainty. Any consideration of your entitlement to extension of time or loss and/or expense on this contract will take such matters into account.

Yours faithfully

Copies: Quantity surveyor
          Clerk of works [*if applicable*]

[[1] *When using IC, ICD, MW or MWD, the underlined part should read: 'at all reasonable times to keep upon the Works a competent person-in-charge'.*
[2] *When using IC or ICD or MW or MWD add: 'at all reasonable times'.*]

K25 Variations: change in scope and character of the work (102)

One of the important reasons for the 'variation clause' (clause 5) is to prevent the contract being put at an end by an instruction to the contractor to alter or modify the Works in some way. Clause 3.14.5 specifically mentions the point. If it were not for the existence of clause 5, a relatively minor alteration would necessitate a renegotiation of the contract. In reality, the clause probably allows quite substantial changes.

Sometimes, if a contractor is falling behind in the programme and/or losing money, it will try to argue that the contract is at an end and should be renegotiated because the variations have altered the whole scope and character of the work. If the variations have had this effect, the contractor would be right in this assertion despite clause 3.14.5. All rests upon what the parties contemplated and expressed as their intentions in the contract.

For example, if the contract was to build one house and you issued a variation to add another similar house, it would probably vitiate the original contract because you have increased the scope of the work by 100% and the contract would be markedly different from that which the contractor undertook to carry out. If, however, the contract was to build one hundred houses and you issued a variation to add one house, it would be unlikely to vitiate the contract because you have increased the scope by a mere 1% and it is the same contract with a minor variation to the work. To get at the principle you must consider that the first contract was doubled in scope but the second contract was increased fractionally.

An extreme case of altering the character of the work would be to issue a variation altering a factory into a school. Such a measure would clearly vitiate the contract. A purported variation instructing the substitution of a highly complicated structure in place of a very simple building probably also falls outside the clause.

You are unlikely to have taken such drastic steps as regards scope or character but you are almost certain to have issued a number of instructions requiring minor variations. The contractor usually bases any case on the fact that clause 3.14.5 refers to variation in the singular. In other words 'no variation' shall vitiate the contract, but *variations* might. It may be argued that the total variations you have issued have, taken together, changed the scope and character of the work. This approach would be correct if your variations had, little by little, altered virtually every detail of your building.

Fortunately, such situations are rare. The contractor would be unlikely to succeed in any action. But you must be firm.

IC, ICD

Clause 3.11.4 (3.11.5 in ICD) also provides that no instruction or sanction of a variation will vitiate the contract, and the comments also apply to these forms.

MW, MWD

Clause 3.6.1 refers to the architect ordering an addition to or an omission from or other change in the Works without 'invalidating' the contract. This is basically the same as vitiating the contract as noted in the standard form. The contractor may still base a case on the singular, i.e. 'an addition' etc. The general remarks are applicable, as is letter **102**.

K26   Postponement: claimed implied in instructions (103), (104)

You are entitled to issue instructions to postpone the work under clause 3.15 of the conditions. The contractor is entitled to loss and/or expense due to such postponement (clause 4.24.2.1). Therefore, you will be reluctant to issue postponement instructions. What is the position if the contractor claims that your instructions on some other matter effectively imply postponement?

Although it is possible that instructions to deal with defective work may constitute postponement instructions, it is more likely that what the contractor is really saying is that your instructions have caused delay, which is quite another matter and may only give entitlement to an extension of time.

Case law suggests that the courts will treat each situation on its merits. Try not to anticipate an adverse judgment. Your best move is to state your position clearly for the benefit of the contractor and the record.

IC, ICD

Postponement is governed by clause 3.12 and any loss and/or expense would be reimbursed under clause 4.18.2.1.

MW, MWD

There are no specific provisions for postponement. The general remarks in this section are applicable but a different letter is required. Letter **104** should be used.

K27   If suspension letter received from contractor (105)

Clause 4.14 of the contract, echoing section 112 of the Housing Grants, Construction and Regeneration Act 1996, entitles the contractor to serve a seven-day notice of intention to suspend performance of its obligations under the contract, if money outstanding in a certificate has not been paid by the final date for payment and if the relevant payment proposal or withholding notices have not been served by the employer. For the contractor to actually suspend performance in this way will have serious consequences for the employer, because the

102
Letter from architect to contractor, if it is alleged the scope and character of the work changed

Dear

[*insert appropriate heading*]

I received your communication of the [*insert date*] and I totally reject any suggestion that the whole scope and character of the work has been changed.

If you persist in this attempt to repudiate the contract, the consequences will be very serious for you.

Yours faithfully

Copy: Quantity surveyor

103
Letter from architect to contractor, regarding alleged postponement

---

This letter is not suitable for use with MW or MWD

Dear

[*insert appropriate heading*]

Thank you for your letter of [*insert date*].

There are specific provisions for postponement in clause 3.15[1] of the conditions.

I have issued no postponement instructions in accordance with clause 3.15[2] or otherwise and I do not intend to do so in connection with the matter to which you refer.

If you wish to make any claims under this contract, you must submit them in accordance with the provisions of the contract, when they will receive proper consideration.

Yours faithfully

Copy: Quantity surveyor

[[1] *Substitute 3.12 when using IC or ICD.*
[2] *Substitute 3.12 when using IC or ICD.*]

104
Letter from architect to contractor, regarding alleged postponement

This letter is suitable only for use with MW or MWD

Dear

[*insert appropriate heading*]

Thank you for your letter of [*insert date*].

I have issued instructions in accordance with clause 3.4/3.6/3.7 [*omit as appropriate*]. My instructions do not imply, nor are they intended to imply, postponement.

There is no specific provision for postponement in this contract.

Yours faithfully

105
Letter from architect to contractor, regarding contractor's proposed suspension

SPECIAL DELIVERY

Dear

[*insert appropriate heading*]

I note that you have written, stating your intention of suspending performance of your obligations if payment of [*insert amount*] is not made within the next seven days.

Your notice is not valid because

[*Add one of the following as appropriate:*]

the letter was addressed to me and, in accordance with clause 4.14, it should have been sent to the employer with a copy to me.

[*or:*]

the employer has sent a valid withholding notice under clause 4.13.4[1].

[*or:*]

the amount has already been paid in full.

[*then:*]

[*continued*]

[[1] *Substitute '4.8.3' when using IC or ICD and '4.6.2' when using MW or MWD.*]

105 continued

If you proceed with your proposed suspension, the employer will incur substantial costs in dealing with the situation, which may involve the engagement of other contractors to complete the Works. Take this as formal notice that the employer will treat any such suspension as a repudiation of your obligations under the contract which will entitle the employer to recover all costs and losses from you as damages for the breach.

Therefore, I look forward to receiving your confirmation by return that you withdraw your threat of suspension and will work regularly and diligently.

Yours faithfully

contractor's obligations do not only include carrying out the work, but also the maintaining of insurance cover.

Even if the contractor is wrong, the immediate consequences for the employer will be severe, although the contractor will ultimately face a severe liability in damages. If the contractor is correct, you should advise the employer to pay in full immediately. If you believe that the contractor is mistaken, you should do what you can to avert the suspension.

IC, ICD

The contractor's right of suspension falls under clause 4.11 in these contracts and the letter is applicable.

MW, MWD

The contractor's right of suspension falls under clause 4.7 in these contracts and the letter is applicable.

K28   Liquidated damages: objections by contractor (106)

If you certify that the contractor has failed to complete the Works by the completion date, the employer is entitled to deduct liquidated and ascertained damages in accordance with clause 2.32.

The contractor will sometimes raise the objection that the sum stated in the contract particulars is not a true reflection of the damage suffered by the employer and it is, therefore, a penalty and cannot be enforced.

There is a great deal of misunderstanding about this particular aspect of the contract. Penalties cannot be enforced; liquidated and ascertained damages can. Because it is notoriously difficult to ascertain damages after the event, and expensive to apply them, the contract adopts the device of agreed damages. Provided that the employer has considered the amount of damages, usually with your advice, and a genuine pre-estimate of the likely loss has been made and included in the bills of quantities (or specification) sent to the contractor at tender stage, those damages can be applied. It matters not whether the actual loss is greater or less. The important point is that the liquidated and ascertained damages were a reasonable estimate at the time the contract was made.

A penalty is something imposed as a punishment out of all proportion to the loss expected, or one sum payable on the occurrence of any one of dissimilar events. For example, if you were dealing with a private house, reasonable damages might be composed of the weekly cost of renting something similar plus additional removal expenses and incidental costs. It might even be the cost of an hotel room, and something should always be included for your additional fees.

Once calculated and put in the contract, liquidated and ascertained damages do not have to be justified to the contractor before they can be applied.

106
Letter from architect to contractor, regarding liquidated damages

Dear

[*insert appropriate heading*]

I have received your letter of [*insert date*] and read the contents with surprise.

Liquidated and ascertained damages are a genuine pre-estimate of damage to avoid just the sort of dispute you are endeavouring to start.

Neither the employer nor I intend to enter into any discussion with you on the subject. I will only confirm that the sum entered in the contract was a genuine pre-estimate of damage.

Yours faithfully

Copies: Employer
           Quantity surveyor

Obviously, the employer must be prepared to justify them to an adjudicator or arbitrator if the contractor decides to take things to that point. Even then, it is only the method of calculation which must be justified, not whether the damages are accurate at the end of the job.

It sometimes happens that you go out to tender without any sum being inserted as liquidated damages. If this occurs, you are not simply entitled to insert a suitable sum in the form of contract before it is signed. The position is that the contractor has agreed to carry out the work on terms, one of which is that there is no amount of liquidated damages in the contract. In order to be able to put something in the contract, it must first be agreed with the contractor. Perhaps an increase in the tender figure would be required. If the employer wishes to be able to sue for such damages as actually suffered, the liquidated damages clause in the contract must be entirely struck out and initialled by both parties.

IC, ICD

Liquidated damages are referred to in clause 2.23. In other respects this section is applicable.

MW, MWD

Liquidated damages are referred to in clause 2.8 (2.9 in MWD). In other respects this section is applicable.

K29   Termination: by employer (107), (108), (109), (110), (Flowcharts 3, 4)

Termination of the contractor's employment under the contract is something best avoided if possible. If you decide, with the employer, that it is to be done, it must be done in the proper way, and the process is fraught with difficulties. However, the party properly terminating the contractor's employment is legally and financially in the best position provided it is done for a sufficient reason. **Flowchart 3** indicates the procedure.

Clauses 8.4, 8.5, 8.6, 8.11 and paragraph C.4.4 of schedule 3 govern termination by the employer. They can be considered in two parts, the *grounds* for termination and the *procedure* after termination.

Grounds for termination

Clause 8.4 is divided into five separate grounds for termination. They are that the contractor before practical completion of the Works:

- Wholly or substantially suspending the Works without reasonable cause
- Failing to proceed regularly and diligently with the Works or the design of the contractor's designed portion
- Refusing or neglecting to comply with a written notice requiring the removal of defective work, materials or goods and thereby the Works being materially affected
- Failing to comply with clauses 3.7 or 7.1 (sub-contracts and assignments)
- Failing to comply with the CDM Regulations

If it is decided to terminate on any of the above five grounds, you must first give the contractor a notice by actual, special or recorded delivery specifying the default (**107**). If the default is continued for fourteen days after receipt of the notice, you may draw up a letter for the employer to send within ten days by actual, special or recorded delivery to terminate the contractor's employment (**108**).

Note that a repetition of the default at any time after the original notice entitles the employer to terminate within a reasonable time without a further fourteen days' notice.

Clause 8.2.1 requires that the notice shall not be given unreasonably or vexatiously. Although your previous conduct may show that vexation is absent, it is very difficult to decide what reasonable is intended to be. It might very much depend on particular circumstances surrounding the giving of notice.

Consider the five grounds very carefully before giving notice:

(1) *Wholly or substantially suspending the Works without reasonable cause*
    This means the contractor stops all of the work or an important part of it and, upon your enquiry, fails to give a sufficient reason. A sufficient reason might be, under certain circumstances, one of the relevant events noted in clause 2.29. You alone will be in a position to decide.

(2) *Failing to proceed regularly and diligently*
    The contractor must proceed both regularly and diligently. There must be enough resources on site to permit regular daily progress to be made so as to hit any target dates in the contract. The progress must be continuous, industrious and efficient with regard to time, sequence and quality of work.

(3) *Refusing or neglecting to comply with a written notice requiring the removal of defective work or improper materials or goods and thereby the Works being materially affected*
    Since this situation can normally be dealt with under clause 3.11 (as has already been seen) termination appears to be the last resort if a potentially disastrous situation is developing.

(4) *Failing to comply with clauses 3.7 or 7.1*
    Although termination could well be appropriate for a serious breach such as assignment without consent, it seems to be the last resort for the lesser breach of subletting without consent.

107
Letter from architect to contractor, giving notice of default

This letter is not suitable for use with MW or MWD

ACTUAL/SPECIAL/RECORDED DELIVERY [*as appropriate*]

Dear

[*insert appropriate heading*]

I hereby give you notice under clause 8.4.1 of the conditions of contract that you are in default in the following respect:

[*insert details of the default with dates if appropriate.*]

If you continue the default for fourteen days after receipt of this notice, the employer may within ten days of such continuance terminate your employment under this contract without further notice. If you at any time repeat such default (whether previously repeated or not) then upon or within a reasonable time after such repetition the employer may by notice terminate your employment under this contract.

Yours faithfully

Copies: Employer
          Quantity surveyor

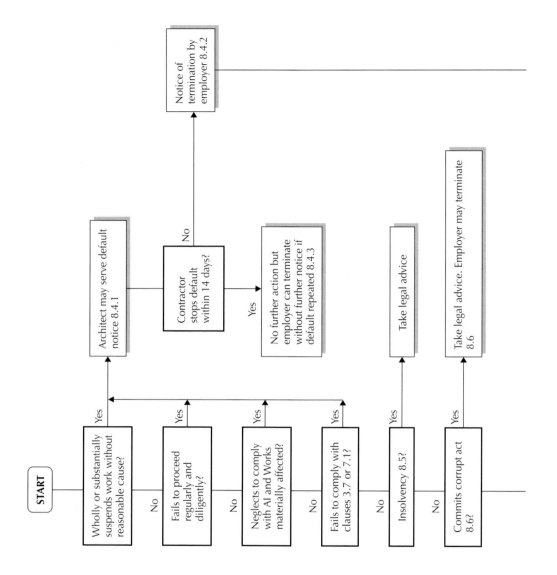

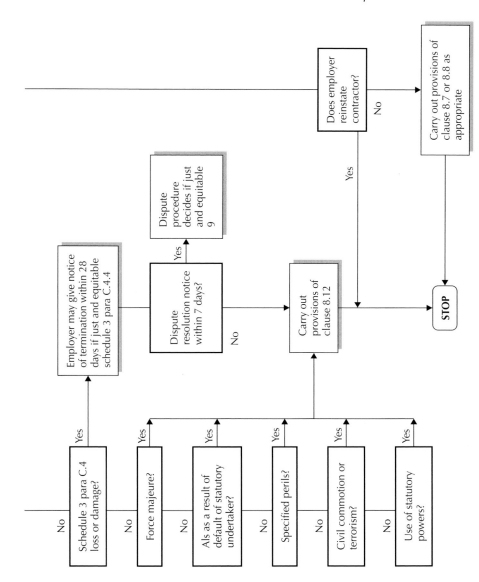

Flowchart 3   Termination by employer under SBC (termination under IC and ICD is virtually identical).

108
Letter from employer to contractor, terminating employment

This letter is not suitable for use with MW or MWD

ACTUAL/SPECIAL/RECORDED DELIVERY [*as appropriate*]

Dear

[*insert appropriate heading*]

I refer to the notice dated [*insert date of original notice*] sent to you by the architect.

In accordance with clause 8.4.2 of the conditions of contract take this as notice that I hereby terminate your employment under this contract without prejudice to any other rights or remedies which I may possess. The determination will take effect on receipt of this notice.

The rights and duties of the parties are governed by clauses 8.7 and 8.8. No temporary building, plant, tools, equipment, goods or materials may be removed from the site until (and if) the architect shall so instruct.

The architect will write to you within fourteen days regarding all sub-contractors and suppliers.

Yours faithfully

Copies: Architect
               Quantity surveyor

(5) *Failing to comply with the clause relating to the CDM Regulations*
The contractual requirement to comply is set out in clause 3.25. Resort to termination would appear to be a remedy available if all else failed to resolve a serious situation.

The two grounds for termination under clauses 8.5 and 8.6 can be summarised as:

- The contractor becoming insolvent
- The contractor being guilty of a corrupt act

In both cases the complexities are such that legal advice should be sought. Indeed, legal advice is always indicated where there is a likelihood of termination.

Procedure after termination

After termination, the procedure is clearly laid down in clauses 8.7 and 8.8, and there is provision for the employer to allow the contractor to resume work if it is thought desirable in the light of events. The contractor is bound to allow the use of all plant, goods and materials on site and, except in the case of certain insolvency events, allow the employer the benefit of any agreements with subcontractors and suppliers. The contractor then has to wait until the completion of the work and all the final costs have been calculated, including any additional loss and expense to the employer. You must not be hurried into arriving at the final figure and, of course, you must work closely with the quantity surveyor. You need not certify any money to the contractor until you are completely satisfied that the employer (the injured party) has been placed in the position, as far as money can do it, he or she would have been in had the contractor's default and subsequent termination not taken place. The employer has six months from the date of termination to decide whether to complete the project. If the decision is that the project will not be completed, an account must be taken to decide the amount owing to the contractor (if any).

Clause 8.11 sets out five grounds on which either party may terminate the contractor's employment. No period of notice is required, but the grounds must have caused suspension of virtually the whole of the Works for a continuous period of the length noted in the contract particulars. The grounds are:

- *Force majeure*
- Architect's instructions issued as a result of the negligence or default of a local authority or statutory undertaker
- Loss or damage to the Works caused by specified perils
- Civil commotion or use or threat of terrorism
- Exercise of statutory power by the UK Government which directly affects the Works

A seven day notice of termination may be given on the expiry of the period of suspension, but it must not be given vexatiously or unreasonably. The grounds can be roughly classified as neutral, i.e. the fault of neither employer nor contractor.

(1) *Force majeure*
The meaning of this term is somewhat obscure. It is wider than Act of God and refers to circumstances beyond the parties' power to control. A war, breakdown of machinery, a strike or fire caused by lightning are examples of force majeure.

(2) *Architect's instructions*
Clearly, architect's instructions issued in these circumstances and which cause a long suspension of work cannot be laid at the door of either employer or contractor.

(3) *Loss or damage to the Works caused by specified perils*
This is self-explanatory, but the clause excludes the contractor's right to terminate under this provision if the loss or damage was caused by negligence of the contractor or any contractor's persons. So, for example, the contractor may not terminate if the loss or damage was caused by a fire started through the negligence of one of the operatives on site.

(4) *Civil commotion or use or threat of terrorism*
This is a situation which falls between riot and civil war. There must be turbulence or tumult present and it may amount to force majeure. Regrettably, terrorism needs no explanation.

(5) *Exercise of statutory power by UK Government which directly affects the Works*
The closure of some paths and roads during the foot and mouth outbreak is an example under this head.

The procedure after termination is the same as if the contractor terminated under clause 8.9 (see section K30), except that it is not entitled to claim loss and/or expense unless the suspension was a result of loss or damage due to specified perils and caused by the negligence or default of the employer or any of the employer's persons.

Termination under paragraph C.4.4 of schedule 3 is open to either party:

- If the contract is for alterations or extensions to existing structures; *and*
- Loss or damage by one of the risks, covered by the joint names policy for all risks, has affected work carried out or materials on site; *and*
- It is just and equitable to do so; *and*
- Termination notice is given within twenty-eight days of the occurrence of the loss or damage.

The question is, of course, when will it be just and equitable to serve notice of termination after loss or damage? A situation which would undoubtedly qualify would be if the damage was so considerable as to effectively destroy not only the executed work, but also the existing structure. Each situation must be judged on its merits and if the extent of damage makes continuance of the contract impracticable, notice can probably be served (**109**). The party receiving the notice has seven days in which to invoke applicable dispute resolution procedures.

The consequence of termination under this clause is generally similar to termination under clause 8.11.

IC, ICD

The procedure is virtually identical to that set out in **Flowchart 3**. Termination by the employer is governed by clauses 8.4, 8.5, 8.6 and 8.11 and paragraph C.4.4 of schedule 1. The provisions are similar although not identical to the SBC provisions, and the above comments are generally applicable.

MW, MWD

Although the general remarks in this section regarding termination are applicable, the grounds and detailed procedure are different. Clauses 6.4, 6.5 and 6.6 govern the position. **Flowchart 4** is applicable. Letters **107**, **108** and **109** are not applicable. Under this contract three grounds for termination are recognised under clause 6.4. The contractor, before practical completion:

- Wholly or substantially suspending the Works without reasonable cause
- Failing to proceed regularly and diligently with the Works
- Failing to comply with the clause relating to the CDM Regulations

As with SBC, these grounds require you to use your careful judgment. Legal advice is always indicated where termination is a possibility.

In the first case, a seven day default notice from the architect, followed by a termination notice from the employer within ten days of its expiry (**110**) by actual, special or recorded delivery is required. Termination takes place when the contractor receives the notice. In the case of insolvency, no prior default notice is needed. The contractor must immediately vacate the site and the employer need make no further payment until after the completion of the Works.

Insolvency and corruption fall under clauses 6.5 and 6.6 respectively.

K30   Termination: by contractor (111), (112), (113), (114)

If the contractor successfully terminates its employment under clause 8.9, the results will be disastrous so far as the employer is concerned.

It is essential that, if the contractor purports to terminate its employment, you apply all your energies to averting the crisis. The contractor will first issue a preliminary notice, either a notice specifying the default or the suspension event, as

109
Letter from employer to contractor, terminating employment after loss or damage

This letter is not suitable for use with MW or MWD

ACTUAL/SPECIAL/RECORDED DELIVERY [*as appropriate*]

Dear

[*insert appropriate heading*]

I refer to your notice of [*insert date*] giving notice of loss or damage occasioned by [*insert particulars of loss or damage which must have been occasioned by one or more of the risks covered by paragraph C.2 of schedule 3 or, if using IC or ICD, paragraph C.2 of schedule 1*].

In accordance with paragraph C.4.4 of schedule 3[1] take this as notice that I hereby terminate your employment under the contract because I consider that it is just and equitable so to do. The rights and duties of the parties are governed by paragraph C.4.4 and C.4.5 of schedule 3[2].

Yours faithfully

Copies: Architect
           Quantity surveyor

[[1] *Substitute 'schedule 1' when using IC or ICD.*
[2] *Substitute 'schedule 1' when using IC or ICD.*]

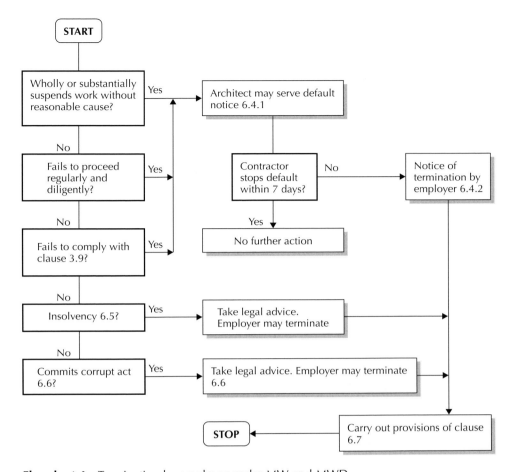

Flowchart 4   Termination by employer under MW and MWD.

applicable. The best thing to do is to take the employer along to obtain special-ist contractual advice without delay. If there is some reason why you cannot do that, there are certain things you can do yourself.

The *grounds* for the contractor to terminate fall into five quite distinct cat-egories. The *first ground*, quite properly, protects the contractor's right to be paid on time. If the employer gets such a notice, payment should be made at once (see item K13). The first three paragraphs of standard letter **74** are appropriate.

The *second ground* provides that the contractor can terminate its employment if 'the employer interferes with or obstructs the issue of any certificate due' under the contract (clause 8.9.1.2). Two points are noteworthy:

● The clause does not refer to financial certificates only. You are responsible for the issue of many other certificates, e.g. practical completion, contractor's failure to complete Works by completion date, making good, etc. It is impor-tant that you issue all certificates at the right time

110
Letter from employer to contractor, terminating employment

This letter is suitable only for use with MW or MWD

ACTUAL/SPECIAL/RECORDED DELIVERY [*as appropriate*]

Dear

[*insert appropriate heading*]

In accordance with clause 6.4.2 of the conditions of contract take this as notice that I hereby terminate your employment under this contract without prejudice to any other rights and remedies which I may possess.

You must immediately give up possession of the site of the Works.

Take note that I am not bound to make any further payments to you until after completion of the Works. I reserve any rights to that time.

Yours faithfully

Copy: Architect

● Interference or obstruction by the employer will be difficult for the contractor to prove because, if it has occurred, it will usually be between the employer and yourself. However, if it came to arbitration the employer may not be able to claim normal privilege for letters which go to the root of the allegation. It should be unnecessary to add that you must resist any attempt by the employer to prevent issue of a certificate (**111**)

In any letter to the contractor you must beware of mentioning the views of the employer in respect of the issue of certificates.

The *third ground* permits termination if the employer does not comply with clause 7.1 (assignment).

The *fourth ground* permits termination if the employer does not comply with clause 3.25 relating to the CDM Regulations.

The *fifth ground* is either of two broadly defined events causing suspension of the work for a continuous period of the length cited in the contract particulars.

Under clause 8.10 the contractor may also terminate without prior notice for the employer's insolvency. Contractual procedures will be the least of your worries in such circumstances.

If the contractor issues a notice of termination before the fourteen days have expired, it immediately ruins its case. The situation does sometimes arise as a combination of a postal delay in receiving the original notice and the contractor's anxiety to terminate its employment as soon as possible. You should draft a letter for the employer to send (**112**).

Each event is subject to interpretation. The only relief for the employer is that the contractor would have to be absolutely sure of its facts, with solid supporting evidence, in order to make the termination stick. In order to deflect the contractor, you would have to do some speedy research to build up a contrary argument (**113**).

If you are unsuccessful in persuading the contractor to withdraw the notice, you must advise the employer that specialist contractual advice is necessary without delay.

If the contractor's termination is found to be valid, the consequences to the employer are grave. The contractor is entitled to be paid:

● The total value of work on the contract fully or partly completed
● Sums ascertained as loss and/or expense
● Contractor's costs in removing all plant, tools and temporary buildings under clause 8.12.2.1
● Cost of materials or goods ordered for the Works for which the contractor has paid or is bound to pay (the materials or goods then become the property of the employer)
● Direct loss and/or damage caused to the contractor by the termination (this will usually include loss of profit)

111
Letter from architect to employer, if attempting to interfere with a certificate

Dear

[*insert appropriate heading*]

Thank you for your letter of [*insert date*]. My comments are as follows:

The contract imposes on me the obligation to issue all certificates at the appropriate time and to use my professional judgment in so doing.

Clause 8.9.1.2[1] of the conditions of contract gives the contractor power to terminate its employment if you interfere with or obstruct the issue of any certificate. The consequences of such termination would be disastrous to the contract.

Naturally, I will bear the legitimate interests of both parties in mind in any decision regarding the issue of certificates.

Yours faithfully

[1 *Substitute '6.8.1.2' when using MW or MWD.*]

112
Letter from employer to contractor, if premature termination

ACTUAL/SPECIAL/RECORDED DELIVERY [*as appropriate*]

Dear

[*insert appropriate heading*]

I am in receipt of your notice dated [*insert date*] purporting to terminate the contract under clause 8.9.3[1] of the contract.

Your original notice of default was received on [*insert date*]. The Post Office will be able to confirm to you the date of delivery. Your notice of termination was, therefore, premature and of no effect. You should already have received my cheque in settlement of certificate number [*insert number*] dated [*insert date*] and, unless I hear to the contrary from you, I will assume that you intend to continue work on this contract in the normal way.

Yours faithfully

Copy: Architect

[[1] *Substitute '6.8.3' when using MW or MWD.*]

113
Letter from architect (or employer drafted by architect) to contractor, if termination notice issued in accordance with clause 8.9.3 of SBC, IC or ICD or clause 6.8.3 of MW or MWD

Dear

[*insert appropriate heading*]

I am in receipt of your notice dated [*insert date*] purporting to terminate your employment under the contract.

I consider that you have no valid grounds for termination and your action amounts to a repudiation of the contract for which the employer/I [*as appropriate*] can obtain substantial damages.

It is obviously desirable to continue the contract without recourse to the dispute resolution procedures if that is possible and I suggest that you should write a letter withdrawing your notice of termination.

It seems that a meeting to discuss your problems is essential and I/the architect [*as appropriate*] will telephone you tomorrow to arrange a meeting of all parties.

Yours faithfully

Copy: Employer/architect [*as appropriate*]

The employer will be obliged to invite tenders (inevitably at increased costs) for the completion of the Works. Delay and increased professional fees will be unavoidable.

If it is decided that there is no defence to the contractor's termination, it is suggested that, with the employer's agreement, you take the following immediate course of action:

- Ask the quantity surveyor to make an immediate estimate of the probable extra cost to the employer, taking everything into account
- Arrange a meeting between contractor, employer, quantity surveyor and yourself

Your aim should be to ensure that the Works are completed as quickly as possible at the least extra cost. Items you will discuss are:

- The contractor's grievances and what can be done about them
- The payment of a lump sum in consideration of the contractor agreeing to carry on with the work
- The withdrawal of the contractor's notice of termination and immediate resumption of work

On the reasonable assumption that the contractor will be content to collect a modest sum without fuss rather than go through the trauma and uncertainty of carrying the termination to completion, agreement ought to be reached. The agreement, of course, is quite separate from the building contract and it must be settled between employer and contractor. No time should be wasted in confirming such agreement. It is best done by the employer's legal advisor. Failing that and as a last resort, you could send a letter (**114**).

Either party can terminate under clause 8.11 or paragraph C.4.4 of schedule 3 (see K29).

IC, ICD

The grounds for termination are similar to those in SBC.

MW, MWD

Clause 6.8 provides for termination by the contractor on any of four grounds:

- If the employer fails to make progress payments by the final date for payment
- If the employer or other person for whom the employer is responsible interferes or obstructs the issue of any certificate
- If the employer fails to comply with the clauses which relate to the CDM Regulations

114
Letter from architect to contractor, confirming agreement after contractor's termination

Dear

[*insert appropriate heading*]

The employer has instructed me to write to you and to refer to the meeting held at [*insert time*] on [*insert date*] at which [*name of contractor's representative*] was present. The following was agreed:

1. [*Note briefly whatever was agreed regarding the contractor's grievances.*]
2. In consideration of you sending the employer a letter withdrawing your notice of termination and resuming work on site within seven days of the above-mentioned meeting, the employer will issue a cheque to you in the agreed sum of [*insert sum*].

Yours faithfully

Copies: Employer
          Quantity surveyor

- If the Works are suspended by either of two broadly defined events for a continuous period of one month

Clause 6.9 provides for termination due to the employer's insolvency.

With the exception of termination under clause 6.9, the contractor cannot terminate unless the default is continued for seven days after receipt by actual, special or recorded delivery of a notice from the contractor specifying the default. The contractor is entitled to be paid:

- The value of the work begun and executed
- Value of materials properly ordered for the Works and for which the contractor is legally obliged to pay
- Any direct loss and/or damage caused to the contractor by the determination

Bearing the above points in mind, the remarks in this section, regarding the serious consequences for the employer, are still applicable as are letters **111**, **112**, **113** and **114**.

K31   Works by employer or persons employed or engaged by employer: contractor claiming that timing not convenient (115), (116)

The contractor may claim that the timing of work to be carried out by persons engaged by the employer is inconvenient. The contractor may be unwilling to allow them on site and threaten a claim for loss and/or expense under clause 4.24.5. A common example of this is when the employer engages his or her own landscapers or painters or persons to construct and fit plaques, sculptures, etc. The contractual position can be found in clause 2.7.

Either the necessary information is provided in the contract bills (or specification) and the contractor should have provided for the work in its programme (letter **115**), or the necessary information is not provided in the contract bills (or specification) and the contractor must not unreasonably refuse to allow the employer to do the work (letter **116**)

IC, ICD

A very similar provision is found in this contract in clause 2.7.

MW, MWD

There is no equivalent provision in this contract.

115
Letter from architect to contractor, regarding work by employer if information is in the contract bills (or specification)

This letter is not suitable for use with MW or MWD

Dear

[*insert appropriate heading*]

I refer to your letter of [*insert date*].

Item [*insert page and item number*] of the contract bills/specification [*delete as appropriate*] clearly states that [*describe works*] are to be carried out by the employer. You included the work in your programme submitted to me on [*insert date*].

You have an obligation under clause 2.7.1 to allow [*insert names of persons engaged by the employer*] to carry out their work at the appropriate time, which would appear to be [*insert date*]. Obviously, the employer wishes to assist you as much as possible but that must be balanced against the employer's other concerns. Probably the best solution would be for you to let me know of a date convenient to you as near as possible to the date in your programme and I will see if the employer will agree.

[*continued*]

---

115 continued

[*Add, if claim is threatened:*]

No claim under clause 4.24.5[1] can be entertained unless all the requirements of clause 4.23[2] are satisfied. It would seem, at this stage, that the employer would have the stronger claim if you were to persist in your reluctance to allow [*insert names of persons engaged by the employer*] on site.

Yours faithfully

[[1] *Substitute '4.18.5' when using IC or ICD.*
[2] *Substitute '4.17' when using IC or ICD.*]

116
Letter from architect to contractor, regarding work by employer if information is not in the contract bills (or specification)

This letter is not suitable for use with MW or MWD

Dear

[*insert appropriate heading*]

I refer to your letter of [*insert date*] in which you expressed your reluctance to allow the employer to execute [*describe work*] on [*insert date*].

I am surprised by your unhelpful attitude which threatens, over a relatively minor matter, to disrupt the good working relationship we have established on this contract.

Clause 2.7.2 requires your consent to the execution of the work but this consent is something you cannot, under the terms of the contract, unreasonably withhold. Please let me know by return why the date(s) proposed is (are) not convenient and which date(s) would be convenient so that I can decide whether you are withholding your consent unreasonably. There must be an element of accommodation in every contract and I trust that I am not misguided in my confidence that this matter can be settled in a spirit of mutual co-operation.

[*Add the following if a claim is threatened:*]

Any claim under clause 4.23[1] will be considered at the appropriate time if it is properly submitted.

Yours faithfully

[[1] *Substitute '4.17' when using IC or ICD.*]

K32   Reference to your 'nominated' subcontractor (117)

There is no longer any provision for you to 'nominate' under SBC. However, many architects invite tenders from sub-contractors and, in effect, nominate the successful sub-contractor by instructing the contractor to accept the tender and enter into a contractual relationship with the sub-contractor. This practice is not recommended and it is likely that the contractor can successfully object to the instruction. However, if the contractor does accept the instruction and comply, the situation is entirely different from that which exists if the employer directly employs persons to carry out work where the employer has control over such persons.

It is, however, very common for a contractor to telephone or write complaining that your 'nominated' sub-contractor is holding up the Works for some reason and what do you intend to do about it? Unless the circumstances warrant your direct intervention, which is usually very ill-advised and probably means that termination is imminent, you should take no action, but send a fairly brief reply (**117**).

IC, ICD

There are no nominated sub-contractors under this form either, but there are named persons as sub-contractors which are similar to the extent that you name them and the contractor enters into a sub-contract with them. The contractor may take the same approach as under SBC and your reply will be similar.

MW, MWD

A similar situation may arise and the letter is applicable.

K33   Sub-contractor: drawings for approval (118), (119)

The contractor will usually submit drawings received from a sub-contractor or supplier for your approval. On the basis that they are not design drawings, but simply produced from your own drawings, it is the contractor's responsibility to check and co-ordinate them. A typical example is a window schedule or a setting out drawing for a staircase balustrade. You must be careful not to relieve the contractor of responsibility. The situation may be more complex if the drawings have some design content which is normally part of your design responsibility.

If the sub-contractor or supplier has supplied drawings directly to you, this type of letter is not really suitable. Try letter **119**. Where the drawings have been submitted because the contractor's designed portion has been used under SBC, ICD or MWD, see K10.

117
Letter from architect to contractor, if your 'nominated' sub-contractor alleged

Dear

[*insert appropriate heading*]

Thank you for your letter of [*insert date*].

Although you are correct in saying that I instructed you to accept the tender of [*insert the name of the sub-contractor*], that does not mean that the sub-contractor becomes a nominated sub-contractor. There is no provision for nomination in this contract. You have a contractual relationship with the sub-contractor in question and you should look to the terms of that sub-contract for your remedies in this instance.

Yours faithfully

118
Letter from architect to contractor, if drawings submitted for approval

Dear

[*insert appropriate heading*]

Thank you for your letter of [*insert date*] enclosing two copies of [*insert name of sub-contractor*] drawings numbers [*insert drawing numbers*].

My comments are as follows:

[*List comments*]

These are not design drawings, but drawings produced from information I have supplied. It is your responsibility under the contract to check and co-ordinate these sub-contractors' drawings required to execute the Works. This letter must not be construed so as to relieve you of that responsibility and my comments are so restricted. I have retained one copy of the drawings for my records.

Yours faithfully

119
Letter from architect to sub-contractor, if drawings submitted directly to the architect for approval

Dear

[*insert appropriate heading*]

Thank you for your letter of [*insert date*] enclosing two copies of [*insert name of sub-contractor*] drawings numbers [*insert drawing numbers*].

The employer under the main contract has no contractual relationship with you and I have no powers or duties under your sub-contract. I, therefore, return the drawings herewith and suggest that, in future, you address all correspondence to the main contractor.

Yours faithfully

Copy: Contractor

IC, ICD

The remarks in this section are applicable to drawings produced by named persons as sub-contractors.

MW, MWD

The remarks in this section are generally applicable to the rare instances where the contractor sends you a drawing for approval. Letters **118** and **119** are applicable.

K34   Arbitration: threatened over a small matter (120), (121)

If the contractor does not agree with your decision in some respect, it may write to the employer to ask for concurrence in the appointment of an arbitrator. It may simply be a threat to persuade you to alter your decision. What you should do next depends upon:

- Whether the item is paltry in financial terms (depends upon the value of the item in dispute in relation to the whole contract and the resources of the contractor) (**120**)
- Whether, irrespective of the value of the item, your knowledge of the contractor leads you to believe that it will proceed to arbitration (**121**). Take care with this assessment and be pessimistic

Points to note are:

- It is thought by some that if the employer concurs in the appointment of an arbitrator, this may tend to give the impression that there is some merit in the contractor's case. On the other hand, the employer's prompt agreement may give pause for thought to a contractor who is simply trying to threaten
- Always try to sort out the difference by a meeting. Most projected arbitrations peter out or are settled before the actual hearing stage is reached
- The outcome of arbitration, like the outcome of litigation, can never be predicted by either party, no matter how strong they consider their case to be

K35   Adjudication: threatened over a small matter (122)

Since the introduction of adjudication in construction contracts, contractors have become more likely to use this dispute resolution route than arbitration.

120
Letter from architect to contractor, if item is paltry or architect does not consider that it intends to proceed to arbitration

SPECIAL/RECORDED DELIVERY [*as appropriate*]

Dear

[*insert appropriate heading*]

I am in receipt of your letter of [*insert date*]. [*If sent to the employer, add:* '*passed to me by the employer*'.]

The step you propose is very serious and tends to be expensive to both sides irrespective of the outcome. Indeed, in the present case the legal and other costs are likely to outweigh any financial advantage many times over. Naturally, I am confident that my decision would be upheld in arbitration. Nevertheless, none of us, as reasonable people, would relish the idea of many months of additional work and expense if it can be avoided.

Perhaps the next step should be a meeting at this office as soon as possible in an attempt to resolve this dispute. If this idea is of interest, please confirm in writing that you withdraw your notice requiring concurrence to enable the meeting to proceed in an appropriate atmosphere.

Yours faithfully

Copy: Employer

121
Letter from architect to contractor, if it is believed that it intends to take the matter to arbitration

SPECIAL/RECORDED DELIVERY [*as appropriate*]

Dear

[*insert appropriate heading*]

I am in receipt of your letter of [*insert date*]. [*If sent to the employer, add: 'passed to me by the employer'.*]

The step you propose is serious with severe financial implications as to costs for both parties. I firmly hold that my decision, which you seek to question, is correct.

Before I advise the employer regarding the appointment of an arbitrator, I suggest we meet at my office to discuss your problems like reasonable people. If you wish to do that, please telephone me to arrange a convenient time and confirm in writing by return that you will suspend the operation of the arbitration notice for a period of, say, four weeks from the date of your letter.

Yours faithfully

Copy: Employer

122
Letter from architect to contractor, if adjudication threatened over a small matter

SPECIAL/RECORDED DELIVERY [*as appropriate*]

Dear

[*insert appropriate heading*]

I am in receipt of your letter of [*insert date*]. [*If sent to the employer, add: 'passed to me by the employer'.*]

I note that you are considering referring [*describe the dispute sufficiently to identify it*] to adjudication. That, of course, is a matter for you to decide. You should bear in mind that the time schedule is some thirty-five days from initiation and that, if you are unsuccessful as we believe will be the case, you will have to pay the adjudicator's fees. Win or lose, you will be unable to recover your legal costs.

Obviously, we are always ready to meet you to discuss the matter.

Yours faithfully

Copy:　Employer

Adjudication is theoretically better suited than arbitration or litigation for small disputes. However, legal costs are not usually recoverable and the loser must pay the adjudicator's fee. Therefore, it is best avoided if at all possible. Try a letter.

Care must be taken that the contractor's letter is not an adjudication notice (or, more precisely, a notice of intention to seek adjudication). That is the first step in adjudication. To be a valid notice, it must be sent to the employer; it must state the contractor's intention to refer a dispute to adjudication and it must specify the dispute and the redress being sought. The employer must seek immediate legal advice on such a notice.

K36   Adjudication: if architect asked to respond on behalf of the employer (123)

Adjudication takes place between the employer and the contractor (and sometimes between the architect and the client), but not between the contractor and the architect. Therefore, if the architect receives a notice of adjudication from the contractor, it has been incorrectly served. Often, an employer who receives a notice of adjudication will pass it to the architect with instructions to deal with it. If you are placed in this position you should refuse to do so. Make sure that you tell the employer in writing.

Architects do not have the necessary expertise or experience to successfully respond to the contractor's referral, especially if it has been drafted by experts. It is highly unlikely that an architect would be covered by normal professional indemnity insurance for negligence in dealing with an adjudication. Even more reprehensible is when the employer's solicitors ask the architect to respond. Obviously, you have a duty to co-operate (at a fee) with the employer's advisers by supplying them with copy drawings and correspondence, participating in meetings and even giving witness statements if appropriate, but you should not take on the job of preparing the response itself. Whatever may have been the intention of Parliament when enacting the legislation, adjudication is not something which can be done by anyone. It is rapidly becoming a specialised undertaking.

K37   Employer: instructions given direct to the contractor (124), (125), (126), (127)

Usually the architect would prefer the employer to stay away from site until the Works have reached practical completion. An employer on site tends to be like a patient supervising the removal of his or her own appendix – a good idea, but only in theory. This is particularly true of professional people because employers, such as lawyers, accountants or physician employers, become more nervous than normal at the sight of building work. However, many employers do make

123
Letter from architect to employer, if asked to respond in adjudication

Dear

[*insert appropriate heading*]

Thank you for your letter dated [*insert date*].

Adjudication is a rapid method of dispute resolution. Receipt of a notice of adjudication from the contractor means that its referral or claim will follow within seven days and the decision will be made twenty-eight days thereafter. Dealing with adjudication is a specialised undertaking which is not within either my field of expertise or experience. Therefore, you should appoint expert advisers to assist you and, in view of the very short timescale, you should make the appointment immediately. If you wish, I can suggest people who practise in this field.

Obviously, I am ready to provide whatever assistance I can to your advisers, for which I would charge an additional fee on a time charge basis of [*insert the rate*] per hour plus expenses and VAT. I envisage that might take the form of copy drawings and correspondence and assisting in discussions.

Yours faithfully

a practice of visiting the site. If the employer does this, never let it be unaccompanied. Make sure, before the commencement of the work on site, that you warn the employer of the problems which might arise if there is direct contact with the contractor. Your letter (**124**) could form part of another letter which you are writing about other aspects of the contract.

Despite the warning, the employer may visit the site without you. What is worse, the employer may give an instruction or answer a query which the contractor puts into effect without consulting you. The position is very awkward. Although you alone are empowered to issue instructions (clause 3.10) under the contract, it is clear that the two parties to a contract, by mutual agreement, can vary any of the terms at any time. In effect, it could mean that the contractor can proceed on instructions from the employer and claim payment.

Whether such instructions are reimbursable through or outside the contract depends on whether the instruction is simply the parties agreeing to vary the terms so that the employer can give direct instructions or whether another little contract has been formed especially to deal with the subject matter of the instruction. Either situation can cause you problems.

Your relationship with the employer is a very delicate and personal thing and you must adjust your letter (**125**) accordingly.

There may be no problem, because the employer may be prepared to stand by the instruction and pay the contractor directly, or to authorise you to ratify it with an architect's instruction so that it can be paid for under the contract.

However, there are some situations which are not so simple. For example, suppose the employer gives instructions directly to the contractor which are carried out and they are not instructions which you would ever consider giving. They may pose future structural or environmental problems. They may give rise to a strong possibility of water ingress, condensation or cold bridging. If such instructions are actually contrary to statutory requirements, whether planning, building control, fire or some other, you can simply inform both employer and contractor that the work is unlawful and that it must be removed.

Even if the work does not actually contravene some regulation, you must think quite carefully whether you can continue to act for the employer, because giving instructions without reference to you suggests a serious difficulty in your relationship. At the very least, you must distance yourself from such instructions and the possible consequences.

It is possible that the employer will ask you to retrieve the situation when the full extent of the consequences of the direct instructions are realised. The employer may possibly say that the contractor was told to consult you before carrying out the instructions or that no instructions were given at all. In these situations, where the client is desperate not to lose face (and possibly money), employer and contractor can easily and quickly get in dispute. It is a situation not of your making. Indeed you have done your best to avoid it. It is not your problem and you should simply take a strict line and, in the absence of evidence, refuse to take any action on the alleged instruction. However, most architects are keen to rescue their clients from this kind of situation, no matter how unwise

124
Letter from architect to the employer, warning against direct contact with the contractor

Dear

[*insert appropriate heading*]

May I offer a word of advice regarding your relations with the contractor? I have the duty to administer all aspects of the above Works in accordance with the contract you have signed. If any employee of the contractor communicates with you by letter, telephone or personal visit, please refer that person to me and let me know immediately. It is not advisable for you to answer any queries or make any decisions regarding the contract without consulting me. This could also be costly. If there are any matters requiring your decision, I will refer them to you, as they arise, with any observations I may have.

I understand that you may wish to visit the site to see the work in progress from time to time. If so, please let me know so that I can make myself available to accompany you on each occasion to take care of any points which may arise.

Yours faithfully

125
Letter from architect to the employer, regarding client's instructions on site

Dear

[*insert appropriate heading*]

When I called on site today, the contractor informed me that you had preceded me and given the following instructions:

[*insert instructions issued by your client.*]

Your instructions have already been put into effect with the result that [*summarise the material consequences*]. Naturally, the contractor will claim appropriate payments, and I informed the person in charge that such claims must be sent directly to you, because they are strictly outside the contract.

It would be in your own best interests for you to visit the site only in my company so that you have professional advice for any amendments you may wish to make.

Yours faithfully

Copy: Quantity surveyor

that course of action may be. If you are determined to tread this path, tread carefully and send a preliminary letter (**126**) to the employer before seeing what you can do with the contractor (**127**).

The contractor basically can only answer yes or no. If yes, there should be no further problems. If no, you must involve the employer fully. The employer got into the mess by visiting the site alone. You will probably give advice bearing in mind that:

- If you issue an instruction in accordance with clause 3.18.1 to remove defective work, the contractor may seek adjudication
- The chances are that the adjudicator would support the instruction under clause 3.18.1, but this is by no means certain because much would turn upon the precise facts of the case as found by the adjudicator
- Your duty under the contract is to issue the clause 3.18.1 instruction

You should encourage the employer to take appropriate legal advice at this stage and you should protect yourself by obtaining precise written instructions on the matter.

IC, ICD

Clause 3.8 empowers you to issue instructions. Instructions to remove defective work would be under 3.16.1.

MW, MWD

All instructions are empowered by clause 3.4.

K38   Employer: additional items forgotten by architect (128)

In almost every contract it is inevitable that you will have overlooked some items at tender stage. You will be involved in issuing instructions to correct the situation.

The employer will not always appreciate that some items will be forgotten. It is prudent to seek approval for what might be termed 'legitimate' extras as they occur (such as items necessitated by the employer's own changes of mind or an unexpected additional expense due to unavailability of material etc.). Items which have been forgotten may be embarrassing, but you must refer back to the employer for authority to expend money. If you adopt a straightforward approach, you should have no difficulty provided that they are not so expensive that they would have pushed the original tender price into the prohibitive bracket had they been included at tender stage (**128**). If that is the position, take advice before proceeding further.

126
Letter from architect to the employer, if asked to retrieve the situation

Dear

[*insert appropriate heading*]

I refer to our recent conversation regarding the alleged instructions which I mentioned in my letter of [*insert date of your previous letters*]. I note that you wish me to retrieve the situation as far as possible and, naturally, I wish to do anything I can to assist. I will proceed on the understanding that you accept that I have no responsibility for the consequences of the alleged instruction nor the consequences of my attempts to retrieve the matter. The contractor could argue:

1. That you varied the terms of the contract; or
2. That your alleged instructions were outside the contract altogether and amounted to another contract.

How far these contentions would succeed could be a matter for an adjudicator or a court to decide.

Yours faithfully

127
Letter from architect to contractor, regarding the employer's alleged instructions

Dear

[*insert appropriate heading*]

I refer to my visit to site on [*insert date*] when you informed me that you had [*insert variation carried out*] in response to a direct instruction from the employer.

[*insert one of the following sentences as appropriate:*]

The employer informs me that no instructions were given to you during the employer's visit to site or at any other time.

[*or*]

The employer informs me that you were asked to seek confirmation from me before carrying out any additional work in accordance with the employer's suggestions.

The conditions of contract provide that all instructions must be issued by me. You are, therefore, in breach of contract. Are you prepared to rectify the situation on site so that it is in conformity with the contract without the necessity for an instruction under clause 3.18.1[1]?

Yours faithfully

Copies: Employer
          Quantity surveyor

[[1] *Substitute '3.16.1' when using IC or ICD '3.4' when using MW or MWD.*]

128
Letter from architect to employer, regarding items forgotten

Dear

[*insert appropriate heading*]

I refer to my brief telephone call of [*insert date*]. I confirm that the following items were not included in the bills of quantities/specification/schedules of work/employer's requirements [*delete as applicable*]:

[*list items not included*]

The items are necessary, therefore please let me have your authority to instruct the contractor to carry out the work/supply the materials [*as applicable*]. The enclosed financial statement shows that

[*then add either:*]

the inclusion of these items is not likely to result in the contract sum being exceeded if some of the savings achieved in other areas are taken into account.

[*or:*]

the inclusion of these items is likely to result in the contract sum being exceeded by [*insert amount*], even after savings in other areas are taken into account. Had the items been included at tender stage, of course, the position would be just the same.

Yours faithfully

Copy: Quantity surveyor

K39   Clerk of works: faulty written directions acted upon by the contractor (129)

Having no power to issue instructions, nonetheless the clerk of works will frequently issue directions. Usually, the directions are concerned with the correction of defective workmanship or materials but sometimes the directions take on more of the character of instructions to vary or do additional work. Similarly, the contractor often falls into the habit of carrying out the directions as though they were architect's instructions. It is well known that, if it was not for clerks of works directions, some projects would grind to a halt. All may be well until the contractor complies with a direction with which you do not agree. If you find yourself in this position there are three points to consider:

- The necessity to restore the situation to your satisfaction
- The understandable, although strictly unjustified, annoyance of the contractor if considerable expense is involved
- The need to maintain the future credibility of the clerk of works

The contractor should not carry out clerk of works' directions unless you confirm them. The other two points are tricky if you are to carry on a good relationship with all parties on site. It is presumed that you have been careful to spell out the duties of the clerk of works at the beginning of the contract. You will have done it at the first meeting prior to the commencement of work and had the item properly minuted. So now you must issue an instruction requiring the contractor to remove faulty work from site. With the instruction send a letter (**129**).

IC, ICD

Although there is provision for a clerk of works under this form (clause 3.3), there is no provision for the issue of directions, not even those which are of no effect as under SBC. It may be that the clerk of works issues directions, of course, even though not supposed to do so, and if that is the case, letter **129** is applicable.

MW, MWD

There is no provision for a clerk of works in the conditions but you might have made provision, in similar terms to the Standard Building Contract, in the specification. If so, this section is applicable.

K40   Clerk of works: verification of daywork sheets (130)

It is common practice for the contractor to deliver daywork sheets (referred to as vouchers in the conditions, clause 5.7) to the clerk of works for verification,

129
Letter from architect to contractor, regarding clerk of works' direction

Dear

[*insert appropriate heading*]

I enclose my architect's instruction regarding [*describe briefly*].

I regret the necessity of sending such an instruction. However, there is really no alternative. When you complied with the direction of the clerk of works, strictly, you were acting in breach of contract although, no doubt, with the very best of intentions to progress the Works as quickly as possible. Perhaps it is opportune to remind you that the role of the clerk of works is that of inspector and, while always ready to assist you with advice and guidance, the clerk of works is not empowered to issue instructions. The clerk of works, however, is a person of considerable experience and I sincerely hope that you will continue to work together in a spirit of mutual co-operation.

Yours faithfully

Copy: Clerk of works

130
Letter from architect to contractor, regarding verification of daywork vouchers

---

This letter is not suitable for use with MW or MWD

Dear

[*insert appropriate heading*]

I should be pleased if you would note that the clerk of works, [*insert name*], is my authorised representative for the purpose of clause 5.7[1] of the Conditions, verification of daywork vouchers, and for that purpose alone.

If work is carried out in accordance with clause 5.7[2], the vouchers should be delivered to the clerk of works not later than the end of the week following that in which the work has been executed. Vouchers delivered after that time will not be signed.

Please note that the signature of the clerk of works on the vouchers is not an authorisation for payment but only a confirmation that the time, labour, plant and materials noted therein are correct.

Yours faithfully

Copy: Clerk of works
         Quantity surveyor

[[1] *Substitute '5.4' when using IC or ICD.*
[2] *Substitute '5.4' when using IC or ICD.*]

sometimes as much as a month after the work has been carried out. The conditions call for the vouchers to be delivered to the architect or the architect's authorised representative for verification not later than the end of the week following the week in which the work has been carried out. Verification is usually carried out by signing the vouchers. If valuation is to be carried out on the basis of daywork, the figures on a verified voucher cannot be reduced merely because the quantity surveyor believes that the work could have been done in a shorter time. However, the clerk of works' signature on the vouchers does not in itself indicate that payment will be made, only that, if payment is to be made on a daywork basis, the figures on the vouchers are deemed to be accurate.

The clerk of works is not your authorised representative under the terms of the contract. Vouchers delivered after time need not be verified and thereby the ground is prepared for a lengthy dispute between respective quantity surveyors, which is something to be avoided if possible. If the vouchers are delivered on time, but for some reason you do not get around to verifying them, it is likely that they will have the same standing as if they had been verified. It makes sense to make the clerk of works your authorised representative in a limited capacity for the sole purpose of verifying the vouchers. If you decide to do so, you should inform the contractor at the beginning of the contract.

IC, ICD

There is provision for dayworks in clause 5.4, in virtually identical terms to clause 5.7 of SBC. There will be a need for vouchers if dayworks are authorised, and a need for prompt checking. This letter will be applicable in those circumstances.

MW, MWD

There is no provision for daywork sheets in this contract.

K41   Consultants: instructions direct to the contractor (131)

It is common to have consultants employed upon contracts, quantity surveyors, structural and service engineers and landscape artists being the most usual. They frequently visit the site to inspect their own work and often give instructions directly to the person-in-charge or even to the specialist firms themselves.

The contract provides for instructions to be issued by the architect alone. The ideal is for you to accompany the consultants on every site visit so that you can, if you approve, translate their requirements into architects instructions. Their instructions are of no effect otherwise. It is assumed that you will have made the position abundantly clear at the first meeting of all parties before the beginning of the contract. Many consultants will adopt the admirable practice of sending any instructions directly to you in draft for your approval and issue.

131
Letter from architect to contractor, regarding consultant's instructions

Dear

[*insert appropriate heading*]

In view of recent events on site, I am writing to draw your attention to the contract provision that the architect is the only person empowered to issue instructions. All other instructions, from whatever source, are of no effect unless confirmed by the architect in writing. The restriction applies to all consultants engaged by the employer upon this contract. You will see that this was emphasised in minute number [*insert number*] of the meeting held on [*insert date*].

If we are to avoid a repetition of the problems recently experienced, you must take care to comply with my instructions only and refer any other instructions, suggestions or directions to me for my decision.

Yours faithfully

Copies: All consultants

What if, despite your precautions, a consultant does issue instructions directly to the contractor and they are not to your liking? The position is somewhat similar to that of the clerk of works (see K39). You can put matters right by issuing an instruction to remove the work from site. You can do this under clause 3.18.1. You must, however, write to the contractor and emphasise the position.

IC, ICD

The position is identical under this form of contract. You can order removal from site under clause 3.16.1.

MW, MWD

It is relatively unusual for a consultant to be employed on this contract, but the section is generally applicable if a consultant is used. Any instruction must be under clause 3.4.

K42   Consultants: problems with builder's work (132), (133)

The consultant is responsible for informing you of all builder's work requirements before quantities are finalised, and you should make sure that you obtain all the work requirements of the consultant in writing or on drawings. It is assumed that the consultant is engaged directly by your client.

As work progresses, minor adjustments should present no problem. If some of the builder's work, constructed in accordance with the consultant's requirements, proves to be quite unsuitable and considerable expense is necessary to correct matters, what is your position? Your client will usually look to you for help.

First, you must resist the temptation to try to make the best of things. Place the responsibility squarely where it belongs – with the consultant. Secondly, if the consultant is unwilling or unable to correct the problem at no additional cost, he or she must report to your mutual client. Eventually, you may be involved in sorting out the problem, but it is essential that you enter that situation without liability. It is one of the reasons that you have ensured that the consultant is directly employed and that you have taken on the commission on the basis of SFA/99 or CE/99.

In the first instance (**132**) you are really asking the consultant to either devise a method of overcoming the problem without additional cost to the contract, or to pay for the additional work.

In your second letter (**133**) you are exerting pressure on the consultant and at the same time distancing yourself from the cause of the trouble.

132
Letter from architect to consultant, if there is a problem with builder's work

Dear

[*insert appropriate heading*]

I refer to the problem on site with regard to [*insert brief details of the problem*].

The builder's work has been carried out strictly in accordance with the details you supplied to me with your letter of [*insert date*]. I should be pleased if you would inform me how the matter can be resolved at no additional cost to the contract. If, as appears likely, it proves impossible to amend the work without additional cost, please report the matter directly to our mutual client, copy to me, and ask for immediate instructions.

[*If the work is urgent add the following paragraph (but not when using MW or MWD)*]

The work is in danger of being delayed, and, if the contractor makes a claim, I shall have no alternative but to request the quantity surveyor to ascertain the amount of loss and/or expense due to the contractor in accordance with clause 4.23[1] of the contract.

Yours faithfully

[[1] *Substitute '4.17' when using IC or ICD.*]

133
Letter from architect to the client, if consultant declines to correct problem or report to client

Dear

[*insert appropriate heading*]

A problem has arisen with regard to the [*insert type of consultancy service*].

The builder's work has been constructed strictly in accordance with your consultant's requirements.

I have asked the consultant to report directly to you on the matter and I should be pleased to receive your immediate instructions.

Any delay to the progress of the Works due to late instructions will entitle the contractor to claim loss and/or expense.

Yours faithfully

Copy: Consultant

IC, ICD and MW, MWD

This section is also applicable to these forms of contract.

K43   Extension of time (134), (135), (136), (137), (138), (139), (Flowchart 5)

K43.1   Awarding an extension if bills of quantities show phased completion and only one completion date in contract

Even if the sectional completion supplement incorporated in the contract is not used, it is not uncommon for contracts consisting of a number of units (housing estates for example) to be treated as for phased completion. This is often done by including a table in the bills of quantities (or specification) showing the various periods by which the units must be complete. For example: 'Blocks A, B and C to be completed within nine, ten and eleven months respectively of the date for possession'. The completion date in the contract particulars is often noted as one date only.

In the example noted above, the completion date in the contract particulars might be 20 July 2005. This would mean that the employer, in the bills of quantities (or specification), intended Blocks A, B and C to be completed by 20 May, 20 June and 20 July 2005 respectively. Because clause 1.3 of the contract stipulates that nothing in the bills of quantities can override or modify what is in the printed form, the employer's intentions are of no effect. There is only one completion date in the contract (20 July 2005), which cannot be overridden.

What is the position if an extension of time is requested? Some architects purport to give extensions to the individual block periods. This is clearly wrong (unless separate completion dates are entered in the contract particulars and the sectional completion provisions are implemented). Points to note are:

- Clause 1.3 gives precedence to the agreement and the conditions over the contract bills (or specification) or the contractor's designed portion documents
- Therefore, as noted above, where only one completion date is entered it is the completion date for the whole contract (e.g. blocks A, B and C)
- However, clause 5.1.2 refers to certain restrictions which may be imposed in the contract bills (or specification) in regard to the completion of work in any particular order

It therefore seems clear that the blocks must be finished in the order A, B, C. However, provided that the contract, as a whole, is completed by the date for completion in the appendix (e.g. 20 July 2005), the contractor will have complied with the contract if block A is finished on 18 July and block B on 19 July 2005.

Therefore, the employer would be wrong to attempt to deduct liquidated damages in respect of blocks A and B on the basis of the table in the bills of quantities (or specification). Even if liquidated damages are expressed as £x per dwelling per week, they are not enforceable. It is meaningless to attempt to give an extension of time in respect of the individual blocks unless the sectional completion provisions are used, in which case it is essential to give extensions of time on the basis of individual sections. The moral is that, if the employer requires certain blocks to be completed by specific dates, the sectional completion provisions should be used and separate dates entered in the contract particulars. This allows each section to be considered individually for such things as possession, completion, extensions of time and liquidated damages.

In the example used above, you would have to consider simply whether the single completion date should be extended.

IC, ICD

The comments above are generally applicable. Clause 5.1.2 refers to restrictions on the order of the work etc. Clause 1.3 gives precedence to the agreement and conditions over the specification (or schedules of work or contract bills).

MW, MWD

It is unlikely that phased completion would be used with this contract and, therefore, this section is not applicable.

K43.2   Failure to fix a completion date within the appropriate time (134), (135)

Architects appear to be notorious, among contractors at any rate, for slowness in giving extensions of time. On the face of it, the contract places a strict requirement on the architect, in clauses 2.28.2 and 2.28.5, to fix a completion date within specific time limits, and, obviously, it is important for you to adhere to the time limits. The requirements fall into two distinct parts:

- Fixing a new completion date as soon as reasonably practicable but not later than twelve weeks from receipt of notice and the required particulars or, if the original completion date would occur before the expiry of twelve weeks, endeavouring to do so before the original completion date expires
- Notifying the contractor, not later than twelve weeks after the date of practical completion, that the completion date is confirmed or amended

You may well argue that it is sometimes impossible for you to give the extension within the time limit set down before the completion date. Your problem is taken into account in clause 2.28.2 which requires only that you endeavour to adhere to the time limit. The contractor may not see it this way and may press you for a decision (**134**).

134
Letter from architect to a contractor who is pressing for extension of time

Dear

[*insert appropriate heading*]

Thank you for your letter of [*insert date*]. I will make a decision on the matter of any extension of time in accordance with the provisions of the contract. Despite endeavouring to do so, in my opinion it is not reasonably practicable at this time.

[*Add the following if appropriate, but not when using MW or MWD:*]

Because you have not yet furnished the required particulars, I require [*insert requirements*] before I can consider the matter further.

Yours faithfully

After practical completion, if you should overlook the duty of notifying the contractor in accordance with clause 2.28.5, you risk the contractor arguing that the completion date, being unconfirmed, is of no effect and that time is at large. If the contractor were able to prove this point, the employer would be unable to recover any liquidated damages for any overrun on the part of the contractor. It would not, of course, prevent the employer attempting to prove actual damage at common law, but that would be a complicated business. You would be in breach of your duty and the employer may look to you for recompense.

Clearly, you should strive to fix the date within the allotted period. If you over-look your duty, it is probable that your power to fix a new date for completion has expired. The very worst position to be in is if you know the contractor is entitled to a greater extension of the contract period, but you are unable to give it. Very often, a contractor will be anxious to obtain a further extension of time, which will be more valuable than arguments about 'time at large' which may need adjudication or arbitration to settle. It may be worth asking the contractor and employer to extend the twelve-week period to enable you to carry out the final review under clause 2.28.5. Any contractual term can be varied if both con-tractor and employer agree (**135**).

IC, ICD

The comments above are generally applicable but there is no requirement in clause 2.19 for you to grant an extension of time within any particular time limit before completion date – simply to make a fair and reasonable extension of time *so soon as you are able* to estimate the length of delay. After practical completion, you must review extensions of time, as under SBC, within twelve weeks and letter **135** is applicable.

MW, MWD

Provision for extension of time is very brief. There is no time limit set but clearly you must give your decision as soon as possible and it is arguable that you must exercise your power before the contractual date for completion or any extension of that date. If the contractor presses you unreasonably, letter **134** is applicable. There is no provision for a review.

K43.3   *Best endeavours: contractor's claim for extra payment (136)*

The contractor is required to constantly use best endeavours in accordance with clause 2.28.6.1. If you are too enthusiastic in your encouragement, the contractor may respond by requesting additional payment as though you had instructed acceleration. In fact, you have no power to instruct acceleration under this contract.

135
Letter from architect to contractor, seeking agreement to extend the review period

This letter is not suitable for use with MW or MWD

Dear

[insert appropriate heading]

Thank you for your letter of *[insert date]*. As you are no doubt aware, my power to carry out a review and make further extensions of time expired on *[insert date]*, twelve weeks after the date of practical completion. I would be prepared to reconsider the matter of extending the contract period, but first you would have to agree with the employer a variation to clause 2.28.5[1] enabling me to do so. If you wish me to proceed, all that is required is for you to confirm the same directly to the employer with a copy to me. I will copy the employer with this letter and your letter will be acknowledged indicating the employer's agreement.

Yours faithfully

Copy: Employer

[1 *Substitute '2.19.3' when using IC or ICD.*]

136
Letter from architect to contractor, if payment requested for using best endeavours

This letter is not suitable for use with MW or MWD

Dear

[*insert appropriate heading*]

Thank you for your letter of [*insert date*].

I will carefully consider any claim for additional payment if it is properly presented in accordance with the provisions of the contract. However, you must remember that there is no provision for acceleration in this contract. You must constantly use your best endeavours to prevent delay in the progress of the Works in accordance with clause 2.28.6.1[1]. That is all I have requested you to do and, because it is an obligation under the terms of the contract, no extra payment is possible.

Yours faithfully

Copy: Quantity surveyor

[*[1] Substitute '2.19.4.1' when using IC or ICD.*]

IC, ICD

'Best endeavours' is included in clause 2.19.4.1.

MW, MWD

There is no specific requirement that the contractor should constantly use best endeavours, although clearly it is something you have to take into account when considering awarding an extension of time, because it is part of the contractor's ordinary duty to mitigate loss. This section is not applicable.

K43.4   Claims for extension of time: procedure before the contract completion date (137)

The main steps in considering a claim for extension of time are set out in **Flowchart 5**. It is basically in two sections: before the contractual completion date or any extended date and after that date.

   If you reject the contractor's claims, for whatever reason, quite a short letter is indicated. If the contractor asks you why you have not given an extension time, you do not have to respond with reasons. It is suggested that you should not give your reasons in writing because:

- Consideration of delay is usually too complex to be explained without a lengthy report
- Anything you write down may be dissected word by word if the matter eventually goes to dispute resolution

   There is now some guidance to be found on the process of estimating extensions of time. The courts seem to prefer an approach which makes use of the contractor's original programme, or possibly the as-built programme, and which inputs delays which you accept as being caused by one or other of the relevant events. There are several computer programs which will make light work of entering delays into the programme and reconciling a complex series of delays. Do not forget that the computer can never give you a perfectly accurate answer. It is only a rough guide even if very complex planning procedures are adopted. However, your award is to be a fair and reasonable estimate, very seldom a precise thing. In giving your extension you must:

- Fix a new completion date
- Allocate the extension as discrete periods to the relevant events
- State the reduction in time, if any, which you have attributed to relevant omissions of any work

Once again, it is unwise to elaborate on your reasoning.

IC, ICD

The above comments are also applicable to this contract. The main steps in considering a claim for extension of time are similar to those set out in **Flowchart 5**.

MW, MWD

The provision for extension of time makes reference to 'reasons beyond the control of the contractor including compliance with any instruction of the architect . . . under the contract whose issue is not due to a default of the contractor'. In deciding whether to award an extension you must take into account everything beyond the control of the contractor. Letter **137** and the general remarks in this section are applicable, but note that in any award you should only:

- Fix a new completion date
- State briefly the reason for your award, e.g. adverse weather conditions

K43.5   After practical completion (138)

After the contract completion date, you must take all relevant events within your knowledge into account even though the contractor has given no notice of them. You have until twelve weeks after practical completion to make your final decision under clause 2.28.5. Since your power to fix a new date for completion ceases at the end of the twelve weeks (assuming that the parties have not agreed to allow you to take longer as noted in K43.2 above), it is wise to write to the contractor immediately after practical completion asking for any further information you require or which the contractor may wish to provide (**138**).

K43.6   If the project manager has agreed an extension of time with the contractor (139)

Some projects boast a project manager. Unless the project manager is also named as contract administrator in the building contract, he or she will simply be the employer's representative without any powers under the building contract other than such powers as the employer has and may have delegated to the project manager. In such circumstances, the project manager has no power to agree or to make extensions of time and you must say so quite strongly, with a copy to the employer. If you are hesitant at this point, you will lose control of the project and you may incur liability as a result of failing to carry out your duties properly. If the project manager purports to be acting on behalf of the employer in making the agreement, this may, if true, amount to a repudiation by the employer of your contract of engagement and you should take legal advice.

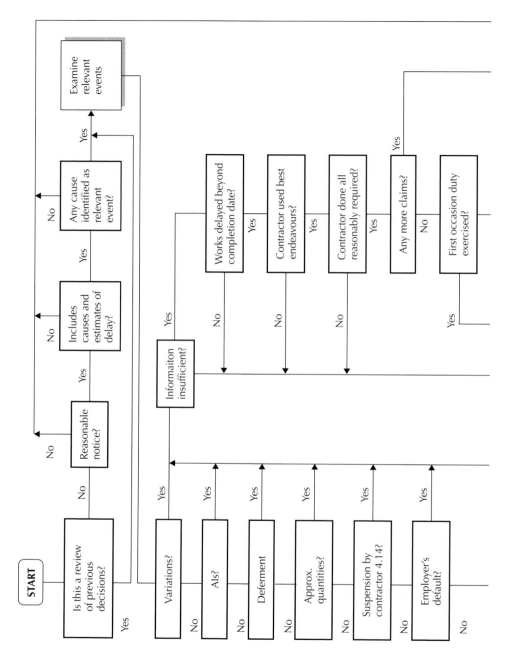

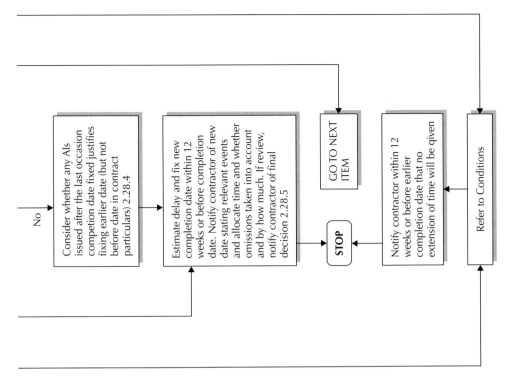

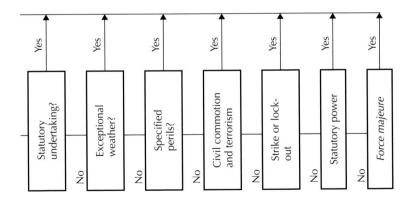

Statutory undertaking? — Yes
No
Exceptional weather? — Yes
No
Specified perils? — Yes
No
Civil commotion and terrorism — Yes
No
Strike or lock-out — Yes
No
Statutory power — Yes
No
Force majeure — Yes

Consider whether any AIs issued after the last occasion competion date fixed justifies fixing earlier date (but not before date in contract particulars) 2.28.4 — No

Estimate delay and fix new completion date within 12 weeks or before completion date. Notify contractor of new date stating relevant events and allocate time and whether omissions taken into account and by how much. If review, notify contractor of final decision 2.28.5

GO TO NEXT ITEM

STOP

Notify contractor within 12 weeks or before earlier completion date that no extension of time will be given

Refer to Conditions

Flowchart 5   Extension of time under SBC (extension of time under IC and ICD is similar).

137
Letter from architect to contractor, if claim rejected

Dear

[*insert appropriate heading*]

Thank you for your letter of [*insert date*].

[*Add one of the following paragraphs as appropriate.*]

Before I can consider your claim for extension of time you must supply me with all the information <u>required by clause 2.27.2[1] of the conditions</u>[2].

[*or*]

I have carefully considered your notice of delay and accompanying particulars and it is my opinion that no extension of time should be given at this time.

Yours faithfully

Copy: Quantity surveyor

[[1] *Substitute '2.19.4.2' when using IC or ICD.*
[2] *Substitute 'necessary for that purpose' in place of the underlined part when using MW or MWD.*]

138
Letter from architect to contractor, before making the final extension of time decision

This letter is not suitable for use with MW or MWD

Dear

[*insert appropriate heading*]

Under clause 2.28.5[1] of the contract, I must carry out a final review of extensions of time no later than twelve weeks after the date of practical completion. In order to do this effectively, I should be pleased if you would supply me by close of business on [*insert date*] with any final information or evidence which you have not presented before and which you wish me to consider in my review.

May I stress two things:

1. For reasons of time, I cannot guarantee to give full consideration to any representation made after the above date.
2. After the expiry of the twelve weeks, my power to fix a new date for completion is at an end even if you provide further important information at that time.

Yours faithfully

[[1] *Substitute '2.19.3' when using IC or ICD.*]

139
Letter from architect to project manager, who has agreed an extension of time with the contractor

Dear

[*insert appropriate heading*]

[*First set out how you became aware of the situation, e.g. 'Thank you for your letter' or 'Following your telephone call', etc. 'I understand that you have agreed an extension of time with the contractor' then:*]

You will be aware that, under the terms of the contract, I am the only person authorised to give extensions of time. That is important, because obviously if another person purports to give an extension of time, it will be a nullity. I should be grateful if you would bear that in mind in the future.

Clearly, the employer is entitled to make direct agreements with the contractor, but if the employer did interfere in areas contractually stipulated to be dealt with by the architect, this would raise serious questions about the architect's future role. Presumably this situation has arisen as a result of a mistake and I propose to carry on dealing with extensions of time and other matters under the contract in the normal way.

Yours faithfully

Copy:　Employer

K44   Claims for loss and/or expense: procedure (140), (141), (142), (Flowchart 6)

The main steps in considering a claim for loss and/or expense are set out in **Flowchart 6**.

There are three basic letters to be sent to the contractor: two if the claim is rejected for various reasons (**140**), (**141**), one if the claim is accepted (**142**). Note that if the contractor does not make its application as soon as it should have become reasonably apparent that regular progress of any part of the Works was likely to be materially affected, you have no power to consider it (see K45). Whether a contractor's application is so late that it cannot be considered is a matter of fact, taking into account all relevant circumstances. There is no magic formula or specific period of time to deal with this, but useful questions to bear in mind in the case of a late application are:

- Has the late delivery of the claim, by its lateness alone, made your consideration or ascertainment difficult?
- Is the employer likely to suffer any prejudice or direct or indirect loss solely attributable to the lateness of the claim?
- If the contractor had made its application earlier, could you have taken any action which you could not take subsequently, to reduce the loss?

Of course, it is almost certain that the contractor will wish to meet you to discuss some aspects of the claim. Not everything can be done by letter.

Basically, before ascertainment can take place, you have to decide on the basis of all the available evidence whether the regular progress of the Works has been substantially affected by deferment of possession or by an occurrence which falls under one of the relevant matters in clause 4.24. Then you must be sure that the contractor cannot recover reimbursement by the application of some other term of the contract. After that, either you, or more usually the quantity surveyor, will carry out the actual ascertainment.

Much has been written about the methods to be employed in deciding whether there is a claim or not. Clearly you may be faced with the protests of the contractor if you reject the claim. How you counter will depend upon the circumstances. Just remember that the grant of extension of time does not automatically entitle the contractor to loss and/or expense. The contractor's claim must be well founded to succeed just as the failure to grant an extension of time does not mean that the contractor has no claim for loss and/or expense. Many contractors try a claim almost as a matter of course. The quality of the substantiating evidence will usually indicate whether a claim is serious or not.

IC, ICD

This section is generally applicable and the steps in considering a claim for loss and/or expense are similar to those set out in **Flowchart 6**. The applicable clauses are 4.17 and 4.18 which outline a simplified procedure to SBC.

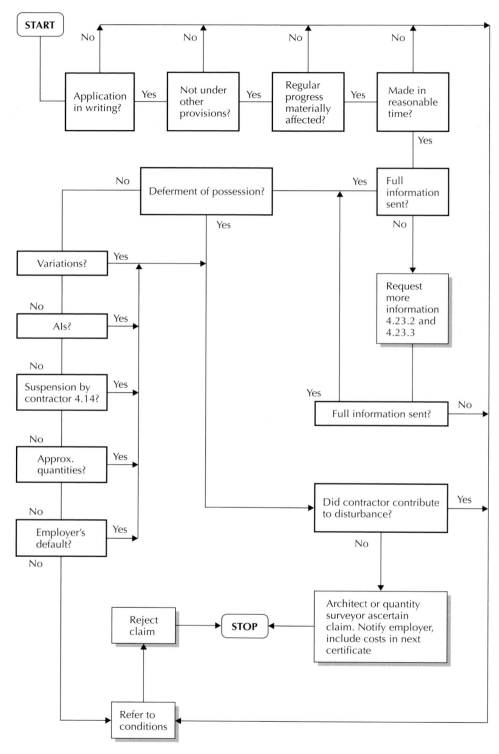

Flowchart 6 Loss and/or expense under SBC (loss and/or expense under IC and ICD is similar).

140
Letter from architect to contractor, if claim for loss and/or expense rejected due to lack of information

This letter is not suitable for use with MW or MWD

Dear

[*insert appropriate heading*]

I refer to your claim for loss and/or expense, under clauses 4.23 and 4.24[1] of the conditions, received on [*insert date*].

Before I can give proper consideration to your claim, you must comply with all the provisions of clause 4.23.2[2].

You have not provided enough information and I attach a list of all the information which I require in order to properly consider your claim.

Yours faithfully

Copy: Quantity surveyor

[[1] *Substitute '4.17' when using IC or ICD.*
[2] *Substitute '4.17' when using IC or ICD.*]

141
Letter from architect to contractor, if claim rejected after consideration of all the evidence

This letter is not suitable for use with MW or MWD

Dear

[*insert appropriate heading*]

I refer to your claim for loss and/or expense, under clause 4.23[1] of the conditions, received on [*insert date*].

After careful consideration of the evidence, I have to inform you that I can find no grounds for ascertaining any loss and/or expense at this time.

Yours faithfully

Copy: Quantity surveyor

[[1] *Substitute '4.17' when using IC or ICD.*]

142
Letter from architect to contractor, accepting claim

This letter is not suitable for use with MW or MWD

Dear

[*insert appropriate heading*]

I refer to your claim for loss and/or expense, under clause 4.23[1] of the conditions, received on [*insert date*].

After careful consideration of the evidence, I am of the opinion that there is some merit in your claim and I am proceeding/I am asking the quantity surveyor [*omit as appropriate*] to ascertain the amount of such loss and/or expense. The amount so ascertained will be added to the next certificate after the ascertainment has been completed.

Yours faithfully

Copy: Quantity surveyor

[[1] *Substitute '4.17' when using IC or ICD.*]

MW, MWD

Clause 3.6 has a provision allowing you to include in any valuation of an instruction any direct loss and/or expense incurred by the contractor due to regular progress of the Works being affected by compliance with an instruction or by compliance or non-compliance with the clauses dealing with the CDM Regulations. This is a fairly limited entitlement not dependent on any application by the contractor although, in practice, doubtless one will be made. If the contractor incurs loss and/or expense due to any other cause, you have no power to consider it. You must refer such claims to the employer. They are essentially common law claims and unless the employer is prepared to deal with them, the contractor must pursue them through the dispute resolution procedure.

K45   Claims for loss and/or expense made months after practical completion (143)

If a contractor has made an initial application within a reasonable time of the occurrence of the relevant matter giving rise to loss and/or expense, there may then be a substantial gap before the contractor provides any further information. This often arrives in a number of lever arch files containing copy correspondence, a financial calculation and some fairly rudimentary arguments. Provided that the initial application has been made on time so that you were put on notice that a claim could be made, you cannot simply reject the submission. You must give it proper consideration.

MW, MWD

There is no claims clause in these contracts and, therefore, the letter is not applicable.

K46   Practical completion: alleged by contractor (144), (145)

In order to secure the release of half the retention money and remove the necessity for a continuous presence of men and plant on site, the contractor will sometimes write alleging that the Works are suitable for occupation, although not every detail is complete and, therefore, practical completion should be certified.

   The certification is a matter for your opinion, but your opinion must be informed by the law. You cannot simply certify or withhold certification on a whim. Practical completion does not mean 'almost complete'. The consensus of judicial view is that the certificate may be issued if there is still some very minor work incomplete, but not if there are any known defects. A useful way

143
Letter from architect to contractor, if claim submitted months late

This letter is not suitable for use with MW or MWD

Dear

[*insert appropriate heading*]

I refer to your claim for loss and/or expense, received on [*insert date*].

It is some considerable time since the events to which you refer. Although you made the initial application within a reasonable time, you have chosen to wait until now to make your detailed submission. Memories of the participants become less clear and reliable as time passes and the ascertainment of loss and/or expense becomes more difficult. The employer must not be prejudiced as a result of your late submission. Therefore, I am entitled to expect that your submission is comprehensive and clear. After it has been considered I will write to you again if I require further information. However, this is to put you on notice that if, after such further information has been submitted, any uncertainties remain, the lateness of your submission suggests that they will not be interpreted in your favour.

Yours faithfully

Copy: Quantity surveyor

of defining it can be that there are no known defects and that the Works have reached a high degree of completion such that the employer can occupy the premises fully, without suffering any inconvenience from workmen putting the finishing touches to the Works. Such a situation might arise, for example, if some of the external works only remain to be completed.

Before practical completion can be certified, clause 2.30 requires that the contractor must have complied sufficiently with clauses 2.40 and 3.25.3, i.e. it must have provided all relevant information reasonably needed for the planning supervisor to prepare the health and safety file under the CDM Regulations and, if the contractor has been involved in any contractor's designed portion work under clause 2.2, a set of as-built drawings and operational information must also have been provided.

There is no reason why you should not note one or two items still outstanding, but beware of preparing long lists of defects at this stage. Contractors should know what is to be done and it is for them to carry out their own checks to ensure that the work is finished and all defects are corrected. If you decide that practical completion has not been reached or if other information is missing, you must tell the contractor (**144**), (**145**).

IC, ICD

Clause 2.21 is to similar effect except that provision for contractor's designed portion as-built drawings occurs only in ICD. Letter **144** can be used with appropriate changes.

MW, MWD

Clause 2.9 deals with practical completion (2.10 in MWD) and the comments for IC are applicable. There is no reference to as-built drawings in MWD as a prerequisite to the issue of a certificate of practical completion.

K47   Practical completion: instructed by the client (146)

Very often, the employer is anxious to take possession of the building and wishes to do so despite your advice that practical completion has not been achieved. An employer will often ask you to certify practical completion so that possession can be taken. Most architects would, rightly, refuse to certify under such circumstances. If the employer insists, to the point of giving you a direct instruction, you should make crystal clear that your professional opinion cannot be changed merely to suit the employer's convenience.

144

Letter from architect to contractor, if practical completion not achieved

Dear

[*insert appropriate heading*]

Thank you for your letter of [*insert date*].

I inspected the Works today and in my opinion practical completion has not yet been achieved. Items are still outstanding. Among other things are:

[*List some of the things you noticed.*]

The above is not a comprehensive list. It is for you to ensure that the Works are completed in accordance with the contract. I expect you to have carried out a thorough check before you again inform me that the Works are ready for practical completion to be certified.

Yours faithfully

Copy: Quantity surveyor

145
Letter from architect to contractor, if practical completion achieved, but certificate cannot be issued

Dear

[*insert appropriate heading*]

Thank you for your letter of [*insert date*].

I inspected the Works today and although practical completion in a physical sense has been achieved,

[*then add either:*]

you have not yet complied with the requirement to provide information reasonably required by the planning supervisor for the preparation of the health and safety file.

[*or, when using SBC only:*]

you have not yet supplied all the relevant information under clause 2.40 for the contractor's designed portion. The following information is missing:

[List]

Yours faithfully

Copy: Quantity surveyor

146
Letter from architect to employer, if instructed to certify practical completion

Dear

[*insert appropriate heading*]

Thank you for your letter of [*insert date*].

I have already advised you that, in my professional opinion, practical completion has not yet been achieved on this project and the contract makes clear that it is my opinion which triggers the issue of a certificate. I understand that you are anxious to move into the whole building, but that cannot occur until practical completion has occurred. The liquidated damages clause is there to compensate you for late completion. Your latest letter instructs me to issue the certificate. Because a certificate is the formal expression of my opinion, I cannot issue the certificate, even in response to your instruction, until my opinion changes. It will not change until the contractor has made considerably more progress with the Works.

By instructing me to issue the certificate you are effectively instructing me to alter my opinion, which of course I cannot do.

Yours faithfully

Copy: Quantity surveyor

L   After Practical Completion

L1   Rectification period: urgent defects (147)

At any time between practical completion and before the expiry of the rectification period, clause 2.38.2 of the conditions empowers you to issue instructions to the contractor to make good any defects (see L5). No doubt you will only do this if the defects are of an urgent nature, but you can issue such instructions as often as you feel is necessary.

   If you have cause to issue several such instructions during the rectification period, the contractor may well protest that you are being unreasonable and that it is losing money. The contractor may suggest that, whereas one such instruction may be justified, the remainder of the defects should wait until the expiry of the rectification period. The contractor's objections are understandable, but if you are satisfied that your instructions are 'necessary' for whatever reason, write to the contractor.

IC, ICD

Clause 2.30 is in slightly different terms and gives you power to notify defects to the contractor not later than fourteen days after the expiry of the rectification period. The effect, however, is similar in that you can issue the instructions at any time during the period.

MW, MWD

The situation is unlikely to arise because the rectification period is normally relatively short and clause 2.10 (2.11 in MWD) is very brief, apparently giving you the power to require the defects to be made good as they arise during the period.

L2   Rectification period: issue of list (148), (Instruction 5)

About a week before the end of the rectification period you should inspect the Works and make a list of all the defects which are apparent and which you consider are the contractor's responsibility. The list may be drawn up in the form of an architect's instruction and delivered to the contractor not later than fourteen

147
Letter from architect to contractor, regarding urgent defects

Dear

[*insert appropriate heading*]

Thank you for your letter of [*insert date*]. Clause 2.38.2[1] of the conditions empowers me to issue instructions regarding the making good of defects whenever I consider it necessary to do so until fourteen days after the expiry of the rectification period.

All the instructions issued in respect of the making good of defects since practical completion was certified have been issued because I considered them necessary. It is not my wish to cause you needless work or expense and any items which can wait until the expiry of the rectification period will be dealt with at that time.

I should be pleased if you would carry out my instructions of [*insert date*] forthwith, otherwise I shall be obliged to issue a notice requiring compliance with my instructions in accordance with clause 3.11[2].

Yours faithfully

[[1] *Substitute '2.30' when using IC or ICD, '2.10' when using MW and '2.11' when using MWD.*
[2] *Substitute '3.9' when using IC or ICD and '3.5' when using MW or MWD.*]

days after the expiration of the rectification period. That seems reasonable, but there are numerous things which can go wrong.

What if you simply forgot to issue a list? Perhaps you drew up a list, sent it for typing and it failed to reappear. For whatever reason, let us imagine that the contractor does not receive your list within fourteen days. What should you do? The first and most obvious action is to issue the list just as soon as you remember. Do it in a perfectly normal manner. There is a chance that the contractor will simply get on with the work (although you are technically in breach of your duty under the contract). The chance of this happening is increased if:

- Your list is only a week or so late
- The defects are relatively minor
- The contractor is anxious to please
- You have behaved in a reasonable manner throughout the contract period

If the contractor writes to inform you that it is under no obligation to attend to any defects which are notified more than fourteen days after the end of the defects liability period, you can write him letter **148**.

The situation is that the contractor's obligation is to carry out and complete the Works in accordance with the contract. If it fails to do this, it is in breach of contract as evidenced by defects appearing during the rectification period. The contract allows the contractor to return to site and put things right. If it does not wish to take advantage of this opportunity the employer is entitled to use common law rights to recover the cost of rectifying the faults. However, this assumes that the contractor has been notified of the defects in due time.

If you have failed to issue the list at the right time, the contractor is still in breach of contract and liable for the cost of making good. However, because you did not issue the list within the time period prescribed by the contract, the contractor has no right or obligation to return and the employer may only recover what it would have cost the contractor to make good. This is achieved by the issue of an instruction in which you instruct the contractor not to make good the relevant defects. This must be with the employer's consent, but following the instruction an appropriate deduction may be made from the contract sum.

IC, ICD

The position under this form is very much the same.

MW, MWD

Clause 2.10 (2.11 in MWD) makes provision for a rectification period. There is no specific requirement for a schedule of defects and it seems that you can require defects to be made good at any time during the period provided you notify the contractor in writing. It would be good practice for you to issue a list, however,

148
Letter from architect to contractor, regarding late issue of schedule of defects

SPECIAL DELIVERY

Dear

[*insert appropriate heading*]

Thank you for your letter of [*insert date*]. I accept that the schedule of defects was delivered later than prescribed in the conditions[1]. However, the situation is that the defects amount to a breach of your contractual obligations. I cannot state that the defects are not present and, therefore, currently I cannot issue a certificate in accordance with clause 2.39[2]. Two important results are that no further release of retention can be made and, similarly,[3] I cannot issue a final certificate.

With the employer's consent, I am entitled to instruct you not to make good these defects and the employer is entitled to employ others to carry out the work and deduct an appropriate sum from any further payments due to you. Take this as notice that if you do not inform me within seven days from the date of this letter that you will carry out the work immediately, I shall advise the employer accordingly.

Yours faithfully

Copy: Clerk of works

[[1] *Omit the underlined part when using MW and MWD.*
[2] *Substitute '2.31' when using IC or ICD, '2.11' when using MW and '2.12' when using MWD.*
[3] *Substitute 'therefore' when using MW or MWD.*]

Architect's instruction 5: Schedule of defects

Defects liability period – schedule of defects

Make good the following defects entirely at your own cost:

[*Insert the list of defects, but not the manner of making good.*]

Please inform me when all the defects have been made good.

Copies: Employer
          Clerk of works

and provided that you are not excessively late in doing so, the contractor has little ground for complaint. **Instruction 5** and letter **148** are applicable.

L3   Rectification period: contractor slow in remedying defects (149)

Clause 2.38 requires the contractor to make good defects within a reasonable time after receipt of the schedule of defects. 'Reasonable' will mean different periods of time in the context of differing contracts. As a rule of thumb, it is suggested that the contractor should normally make a start within two weeks of receiving the schedule. It may well be reasonable to expect all defects to be made good within a month, depending on their nature and extent. No precise guidance can be given. If you decide that the contractor is carrying out its work with unacceptable dilatoriness, you must make your view clear.

IC, ICD and MW, MWD

Defects are dealt with by clause 2.30 under IC and ICD, clause 2.10 under MW and clause 2.11 under MWD. Although there is no specific provision for the contractor to make good defects within a reasonable time, such a provision must be implied, otherwise the contractor could take years over the process. Letter **149** is applicable.

If the contractor's work does not improve, you will have to carry out your threat (see K16).

L4   Rectification period: contractor claims some items are not defects (150)

The contractor may well dispute some items in your schedule of defects. Clause 2.38 states the contractor's responsibilities. Provided that the items are defects, shrinkages or other faults similar to defects and shrinkages and are due to either materials or workmanship not being in accordance with the contract, or the contractor failing to comply with its obligations in the contractor's designed portion, the contractor is liable to make them good.

It sounds straightforward but, in practice, it is all too easy to get involved in fruitless argument. Sit down and think about the contractor's points. If you decide that it is correct, concede the items with good grace. If you decide that it is wrong, make your decision equally clear.

IC, ICD

Clause 2.30 deals with defects liability. The remarks in this section are generally applicable.

149
Letter from architect to contractor, if slow in making good defects

Dear

[*insert appropriate heading*]

I draw your attention to my instruction number [*insert number*] dated [*insert date*] containing a schedule of defects. It is my opinion that you are not making good the defects within a reasonable time.

If your progress does not improve forthwith, you will oblige me to issue a notice requiring compliance with my instruction in accordance with clause 3.11[1].

Yours faithfully

[1 *Substitute '3.9' when using IC or ICD and '3.5' when using MW or MWD.*]

MW, MWD

Clause 2.10 (2.11 in MWD) makes similar provisions and the remarks in this section are generally applicable, as is letter **150**.

L5   Rectification period: employer's refusal to allow making good (151), (152), (153)

In certain circumstances the employer may refuse to allow the contractor to make good defects in some areas which would cause considerable upheaval to the employer's activities. This is perfectly understandable from the employer's point of view. The contract provides that, with the employer's consent, you may instruct the contractor not to make good certain defects and an appropriate deduction is to be made from the contract sum. You should not consider such action if the defects in question are serious. If you consider the defect must be put right, you must write to the employer; do not simply telephone (**151**). In the case of minor defects the employer must send you a waiver of rights under the contract in very clear terms (**152**). The employer may be under the impression that the cost of getting the defects remedied by others can be deducted from the contract sum, although that would be more than it would cost the contractor to do the work. In that, the employer is mistaken and you must make that clear in writing (**153**).

IC, ICD

This section is applicable to this form of contract.

MW, MWD

This section is applicable although the provisions of clause 2.10 and 2.11 respectively are not as detailed as under the other forms.

L6   Final certificate: contractor demands issue (154)

For various reasons, the contractor may write demanding the issue of the final certificate, and you may not be ready to comply. Clause 4.15.1 stipulates that the final certificate shall be issued not later than two months dating from:

- The end of the rectification period; *or*
- The date of the certificate of making good; *or*
- The date the architect sent the contractor a copy of the ascertainment and statement of adjustments to the contract sum, whichever is the latest.

150
Letter from architect to contractor, if it disputes items in the schedule of defects

Dear

[*insert appropriate heading*]

Thank you for your letter of [*insert date*]. Having carefully considered the points you raise,

[*Add either:*]

I am satisfied that every item you mention is a defect, shrinkage or other fault due to materials or workmanship not being in accordance with the contract or your failure to comply with your obligations under the contractor's designed portion[1].

[*Or:*]

I can see the merit in some of what you say. Therefore, I enclose a copy of the schedule of defects indicating the items which I agree should not have been included and which you are not required to make good.

Yours faithfully

[[1] *Omit the underlined portion when using IC or MW.*]

151
Letter from architect to an employer who refuses to allow defects to be made good

Dear

[*insert appropriate heading*]

I understand that you do not require the contractor to make good the following defects because its activities would seriously disrupt your operations:

[*List the defects that the employer does not require making good.*]

Although the contract allows me to instruct the contractor not to make good provided that I have your consent, the defects in question are more than merely cosmetic and, if not rectified, the consequences will be serious. In the circumstances, I should not be carrying out my professional duties properly if I issued such an instruction.

The defects must be corrected. This is an important matter and I will visit you on [*insert date*] at [*insert time*] to discuss the implications in greater detail. Please let me know if that arrangement is not convenient.

Yours faithfully

152
Letter from architect to employer, requiring waiver

Dear

[*insert appropriate heading*]

I understand that you do not require the contractor to make good the following defects because its activities would seriously disrupt your own operations:

[*List the defects that the employer does not require making good.*]

The contract allows me to instruct the contractor not to make good provided I have your consent. I am prepared to give such instruction, but I must have your written confirmation of the following:

1. You do not require the contractor to carry out any making good of the defects listed above.
2. You waive any rights you may have against any persons in regard to the items listed as defects in the above-mentioned list of defects and which have not been made good.
3. You indemnify me against any expense, liability, loss, claim or proceedings whatsoever in connection with or as a result of any or all of the above-listed defects not being made good.

Yours faithfully

153
Letter from architect to employer who wants to deduct cost of making good by others

Dear

[*insert appropriate heading*]

Following our meeting/telephone conversation [*as appropriate*] on [*insert date*], it occurred to me that it may be useful for you to have a written explanation of the 'appropriate deduction' for defects you have decided not to have made good.

On the basis that all defects are breaches of contract and that you are entitled to damages, you must try to mitigate your loss. The defects liability provisions are in the contract to give the contractor the opportunity to put defects right itself. That is obviously cheaper than getting another contractor to do the work. If you opt not to allow it to make good, the contract only allows you to have the benefit of the contractor's own costs. In other words, you cannot penalise the contractor for your own decision.

If you had decided not to allow the contractor to make good simply because its workmanship had been so appallingly bad that you had lost all confidence in it, you would be entitled to the cost of paying another contractor, but that is not the situation here.

I hope that helps to explain the position.

Yours faithfully

The end of the rectification period appears to apply only when there is no schedule of defects – a very unusual situation. The commonest reason for apparent delay is because the contractor is slow in providing the information in accordance with clause 4.5.1 for adjustment of the contract sum. You must make your position clear. It should be remembered, however, that the contractor's failure to supply information does not relieve you of your duty to issue the final certificate. Therefore, if the information is not provided fairly quickly, you should proceed and issue the certificate in an amount calculated without the benefit of the contractor's submission. The contractor's agreement to the finally adjusted contract sum is not a contractual requirement.

IC, ICD

Clause 4.14.1 stipulates that the final certificate must be issued within twenty-eight days of:

- The issue of a certificate of making good; *or*
- The sending of computations of the adjusted contract sum to the contractor, whichever is the latest.

MW, MWD

The contractor may write demanding issue of the final certificate and you may not be ready to comply. Clause 4.8.1 stipulates that the final certificate shall be issued within twenty-eight days of the receipt of all the contractor's documentation reasonably required for the computation of the amount to be finally certified; always provided that you have issued the certificate of making good. The contractor must supply such documentation within such period as is noted in the contract particulars of the date of practical completion.

The usual reason for delay in issuing the final certificate is lack of the necessary documents. Letter **154** is applicable.

L7   Employer: overspending notification (Fig. 3)

This is the subject of many headaches. How to tell the employer that the building has cost more than expected? If you have kept the employer informed, on a regular basis, the final account should not come as a shock and, given the in-built pessimism of most quantity surveyors during the progress of the Works, it might be a nice surprise. If the overspend is almost entirely due to the employer requiring additional items or an enhanced specification and if you have diligently warned the employer of the increasing cost after each such request, you should have no difficulties.

Psychology is important. Your statement to the employer showing the final account should be straightforward, clear and brief. Arrange the various items so

154
Letter from architect to contractor, declining to issue the final certificate

Dear

[*insert appropriate heading*]

Thank you for your letter of [*insert date*]. I am unable to issue the final certificate because

[*Use the appropriate following phrase:*]

you have not yet completed the making good of defects in accordance with clause 2.38[1].

[*Or:*]

I have/the quantity surveyor has [*use appropriate expression*] not yet received all the necessary documentation in accordance with clause 4.5.1[2]. When you have fulfilled your obligations I will issue the final certificate.

Yours faithfully

Copy: Quantity surveyor

[[1] *Substitute '2.30' when using IC and ICD, '2.10' when using MW and '2.11' when using MWD.*
[2] *Substitute '4.5' when using IFC 98 and '4.5.1.1' when using MW 98.*]

Contract sum	£	
<u>Deduct</u> contingencies	£	
<u>Add</u> sundry additional work (brief details)	£_____	
	£	
<u>Add</u> (or <u>deduct</u>) adjustment of PC and provisional sums	£	
<u>Add</u> (or <u>deduct</u>) adjustment of measured work	£_____	
	£	
<u>Add</u> fluctuations	£_____	
	£	
<u>Add</u> reimbursement of loss and/or expense	£_____	
<u>Final amount</u>	£_____	

Fig. 3   Statement of final account to employer.

that the cause of the overspending can be easily seen. Above all, do not make the mistake of being apologetic about it. Unless you have made some gigantic mistake, the employer is getting value for money. Most people are reasonable and, provided you do not lead the employer to think that you are trying to keep something secret, he or she should have no complaints (**Fig. 3**).

IC, ICD

This section is also applicable to this contract.

MW, MWD

This section is applicable, with the appropriate statement of final account, except for the reference to the quantity surveyor who will rarely be used on this type of contract.

L8   As-built records, if contractor or sub-contractor will not supply (155)

It is assumed that you have inserted a requirement in the contract documents that the contractor must supply 'as-built' records at the end of the job and that similar requirements have been inserted in the sub-contract specifications. This should be quite separate and additional to any contractual requirement under clause 2.40 in respect of the contractor's designed portion. Such records serve a very useful function in the future maintenance of the building and may form part of the health and safety file, it being recognised that the finished building

155
Letter from architect to contractor, requiring 'as-build' records

Dear

[*insert appropriate heading*]

Thank you for your letter of [*insert date*]. I recognise that the preparation of 'as-built' records is a tedious procedure. However, these records are vital for the proper maintenance of the building and they are clearly required in the contract documents.

[*Indicate position in documents by reference to bills of quantities or specification and page numbers.*]

You are deemed to have included for them in the overall tender figure and I must insist that you provide them. Depending on the quality of your own records, this may involve you in contacting the appropriate sub-contractors.

Please inform me, during the next week, of the date on which I can expect to receive a full set of the drawings. It need hardly be stated, I trust, that you must bear full responsibility for the completeness and accuracy of such drawings.

Yours faithfully

may differ from the original drawings in important and often invisible respects. It is particularly true of drainage, heating and electrical services.

The contractor should keep records of the work as it progresses. The preparation of 'as-built' records at the end of a job is a tedious procedure which the contractor may try to avoid, even though it should have included the cost in its price. If the contractor makes objection you must spell it out.

IC, ICD, MW and MWD

ICD has a specific requirement for as-built drawings in respect of the contractor's designed portion in clause 2.32.

L9   Defects after final certificate: latent defects (156), (157)

Defects which become apparent after the final certificate has been issued will probably be referred to you by the employer in the first instance. If the employer actually accuses you of, or implies, negligence, consult your solicitor and inform your insurers. If the employer is simply notifying you and asking for help, go and have a look. Your inspection might indicate a latent defect on the part of the contractor.

It is obviously in your interests to be involved from the outset in any investigation and rectification of defects, but do not fall into the trap of doing large amounts of additional work without payment (**156**). Assuming the employer wishes you to deal with the matter and will pay your fees, write to the contractor (**157**).

The contractor will usually agree to inspect but it may disclaim responsibility. You must explain that, if it does not carry out remedial work, the employer will take action at common law to obtain redress. Of course, you may simply get a solicitor's letter in reply to your letter to the contractor. If so or if the contractor just refuses to do the remedial work, advise the employer to obtain specialist legal advice; if necessary, arrange for it and be present when it is given. The implications of defects at this stage are so complex that you should carefully consider the following points:

● You issued the final certificate and it is conclusive evidence that where you have particularly called for the quality of workmanship, goods or materials to be to your satisfaction, whether by reference on drawings, in the bills of quantities or in an instruction, they are to your satisfaction. This is not the same as certifying that the Works are in every way correct. Indeed, it simply means that things which you have expressly reserved for your approval are approved. Moreover clause 1.10.1.1 states that the final certificate is not conclusive that any workmanship, goods or materials comply with any other requirement of the contract. It could be significant, however, if you have reserved for your approval the very thing which now proves defective

156
Letter from architect to the employer, regarding latent defects

Dear

[*insert appropriate heading*]

Thank you for your letter of [*insert date*].

I inspected the [*specify what you inspected*] today and, at first sight and without doing any investigation, it appears that [*insert your initial conclusions*]. However, this view may change when I have had a longer opportunity to examine the problem in depth.

The original contractor should be involved. I shall be happy to deal with the matter for you if you wish and a copy of the RIBA Standard Form of Agreement for the Appointment of an Architect (SFA/99) is enclosed, together with details of the fees and expenses which I would charge. If you wish me to proceed, please let me have your written confirmation of agreement to these terms, fees and expenses.

Yours faithfully

157
Letter from architect to contractor, regarding latent defects

Dear

[*insert appropriate heading*]

The employer has asked me to inspect a defect in the above work which became apparent on or about [*insert the date as near as possible*].

Having carried out a preliminary inspection, my opinion is that the defect is your responsibility. I should be pleased if you would telephone me as soon as possible to arrange a joint inspection.

Yours faithfully

- Is the defect such as you ought to have noticed during your inspections of the work?
- Could the defect be attributed to a design deficiency? If so, is it your design or that of a consultant, the contractor, sub-contractor or supplier? The contractor has limited design responsibility to the employer under this form of contract, and then only if the provisions for the contractor's designed portion are used. If the contractor has, in fact, carried out the design of the defective item, it may be because you failed to do so. Such a situation commonly occurs when an architect does not completely detail something and the contractor, trying to make progress, thinks it knows what is required and presses on. It may be that, in certain specific instances, the contractor assumes a design responsibility in such circumstances, but in general you owe the employer a duty to design the Works and the duty is one which you cannot delegate to someone else without the employer's express authority. The situation with sub-contractors or suppliers is that they owe no design duty to the contractor, but they can be put in contractual relationship with the employer by the completion of collateral warranties. It is essential to do so and also to obtain the employer's authority to delegate any design responsibility

If you are in doubt, you should get expert advice regarding any liabilities you might have and the best way to deal with them.

IC, ICD

In general, the remarks in this section also apply to this form of contract. There is provision for giving the contractor formal design responsibility for part of the work under ICD. There are named persons as sub-contractors and the employer can pursue the named person directly under warranty ICSub/NAM/E.

MW, MWD

The remarks in this section under IC, ICD are generally applicable and there is provision for giving the contractor formal design responsibility for part of the work under MWD, but it should be noted that the final certificate is not conclusive at all and there is no provision for named sub-contractors nor collateral warranties.

M   Feedback

M1   Complaints from client (158)

Feedback from completed jobs is an important method of checking procedures and the performance of the finished building in use. Many architects send a questionnaire to clients at this stage. Some architects consider this is inviting trouble. Much, of course, will depend upon the particular clients and their attitude to life. Generally the client, particularly if it is one for whom you carry out regular commissions, will be very pleased that you care about your work and will recognise that your motive is to improve your service.

Occasionally, however, the feedback comes in the form of a complaint. If latent defects are indicated, you should proceed as in L10. If the complaints are of a more general nature, perhaps related to the working of the building rather than a constructional problem, you should write a friendly letter and follow it with a personal visit. Then you can discuss the precise nature of the complaint, which may arise from a variation in the way that the building is used now that it is occupied.

158
Letter from architect to client, if complaining about the building use

Dear

[*insert appropriate heading*]

Thank you for your letter of [*insert date*].

I always endeavour to carry out a feedback exercise after a project has been completed. I have found it useful for ironing out any problems that may arise after the building has been in use for a period.

I am grateful for your response, which is most interesting, and suggest that I should call and see you within the next few days to discuss the various points you raise. I shall be free [*indicate free dates*] and I should be grateful if you would telephone and let me know which date is most convenient for you.

Yours faithfully

Appendix 1

How to write letters

1.01   Introduction

Most architects have chosen their profession because they have an overwhelming desire to create buildings. Many architects are also accomplished artists. Most want to spent their time creating images of buildings, in whatever medium, and eventually to see their creations in relatively permanent form in concrete or stone or brick, aluminium, glass etc. The reality is that architects spend a great deal of their time not drawing but writing; writing letters and reports. In view of the fact that so much of an architect's time is spent writing letters, it is surprising that very little guidance is given on this difficult subject during the average architectural course. It is usually left for the newly qualified architect to pick up the art of letter writing as he or she progresses through various offices, assisted or hindered by advice from more experienced colleagues.

   Clearly, no amount of teaching and practice in schools could create the real conditions found in practice with their endless diversity. Practice makes perfect and there is no substitute for experience, but some form of guidance may be useful and what follows can be considered useful hints.

1.02   What to say and how to say it effectively in writing

Before you write any letter ask yourself:

- Is the letter really necessary?
- What is it that I want to say?

The sort of letter it is always necessary to write includes:

- Confirming oral conversations
- Answering questions
- Giving information
- Requesting information

Most letters fall into one or other of these categories and sometimes embrace several at once.

One of the commonest faults is to begin to write a letter without clearly knowing what you are going to say. Dictation is a difficult art to master for this reason and it is best avoided, not only by young architects but also by the more experienced. A dictated letter is usually easy to spot because there will be parts of it which are difficult to understand and parts which may not make sense.

The reason for this is that when we speak aloud (as we do in dictation) we automatically emphasise certain words and that helps to give sense to the words. However, when those same words are typed out, there is no emphasis and some or all of the meaning may be lost. The written words must be read carefully by the writer to ensure that there is no ambiguity. There is a well-known joke about the referee who wrote about the job applicant: 'You will be indeed fortunate to get Ms X to work for you'. Clearly that is a sentence with two possible meanings. Moreover, the dictator cannot keep referring to what he or she has already written without much complex pressing of buttons. Therefore, dictation seldom saves time, even for the writer, because there is usually a follow up letter or telephone call to clarify the ambiguities.

Unless your letter is a 'one-liner', always make notes. Ensure that your notes cover all the points and then put them in the order in which you wish to include them in your letter. Usually, if it is a long letter, put generalities at the beginning or the end (but not both) and reserve the bulk of the letter for specifics. It is good practice to number the items so that the recipient can simply refer to the numbers when answering. Some very long letters are better written as a short report.

Keep your sentences short. Re-read your draft to make sure that you have made yourself absolutely clear. Communication is a difficult art. Avoid seeming apologetic if you have nothing for which to apologise. Phrases such as 'I regret' may be acceptable in some circumstances but avoid 'I am sorry to say'. The difference may seem slight but it is there nonetheless. If you apologise, there is the implication that you have been wrong and, therefore, that you may be liable for something. There may be insurance implications.

Architects are often accused of arrogance. The accusers, needless to say, are generally contractors. There is, however, a measure of truth in the accusation in that architects may often seem arrogant if their letters are viewed through the eyes of a contractor. Try not to fall into that trap. Remember that one day your letters may be evidence before an adjudicator, arbitrator or judge. The issue may turn on whether you have acted reasonably in making a decision. Reasonable decisions are made by reasonable men who, in turn, write reasonable letters or so the theory goes. If your letters appear arrogant to a third party, are you likely to be thought capable of making a reasonable decision? Similarly, do not give vent to annoyance. Be totally reasonable even if unyielding in your point of view. The fictitious exchange in letters **159** and **160** illustrates the point.

1.03 Answering letters: the art of isolating the main points

You will sometimes receive letters which are quite simply a confused mess. How are they to be answered?

159
Letter from contractor, to architect

Dear Sir

[*insert appropriate heading*]

I have received your letter of [*insert date*] and view the contents with dismay, bordering on disgust.

Seldom has my company had to deal with an architect who conducts business in so high-handed and arrogant a manner.

I have always strived for a good working relationship in the current partnering spirit, but it would seem that you do not share that view.

If you do not reconsider your decision, adjudication is the next step.

Yours faithfully

160
Letter from architect, to contractor

Dear Sir

[*insert appropriate heading*]

Thank you for your letter of [*insert date*].

It is unfortunate that you do not agree with the decision expressed in my earlier letter of [*insert date*] and have chosen to express your disappointment in those terms. The decision was reached after careful consideration and there appear to be no grounds for altering it. Any further representations you care to make on any point in connection with the contract will receive my careful attention provided that they are accompanied by appropriate substantiation.

I sincerely trust that the good working relationship achieved on this contract will endure for the benefit of all parties.

Yours faithfully

The first thing to do is to decide why the letters are so confused. Is it because the person writing lacks the basic clear writing skills or is it a deliberate attempt to confuse the issues? Your own knowledge of the person concerned will be a major factor in your conclusions. If in doubt, it is always safer to assume a deliberate attempt at confusion. Some architects answer such letters by, in effect, answering the letters the contractors should have written. This is not the correct approach. You are doing just what your correspondent wants – asking your own questions and answering them.

A safer way is first of all to list the points you have to answer; no matter that they are confused in the letter. For example, if the letter refers to extensions of time coupled with breaches of contract and the site agent's impending holiday, all in one muddled sentence, your letter should treat them one at a time, briefly. Devote one sentence to each and avoid linking events together yourself unless your correspondent has done so in a very clear way.

Another method of getting at the nub of the letter is to identify and answer just one point from the letter but be careful to state that the remainder of the letter 'is not understood'.

It may be a painstaking business but over a series of exchanges you should be able gradually to sort out precisely what the other party is saying.

1.04 Obscurities: on both sides

There will be occasions when you do not understand at all what your correspondent is trying to say. Do not be afraid to write back and say precisely that. Do not make assumptions about a meaning. That may be just what your correspondent wants you to do. Many clients are particularly guilty in this respect. They may find it difficult to make important decisions and they would rather you made the decisions so that you can take the blame if they have second thoughts. If you write to your client asking for a decision between granite and hardwood in a particular location, you do not want to read: 'All as we agreed' or 'Granite is my particular choice but the other members of the Board prefer hardwood'. What you want to read is: 'Please specify granite'. Press until you receive a clear response.

It is best to avoid obscurity in your own letters. Although some people do write, as a matter of policy almost, so that their letters can be read in two completely different ways, it is wise to strive for clarity. Deviously obscure letters can rebound on the writer. In this connection, always read other people's letters carefully. They may not actually mean what they appear to say at first glance.

1.05 Points to bear in mind

- It is always a good idea to write your letters thinking that, one day, they will be read out in court
- If you simply acknowledge receipt of a letter you may be implying that you agree with its contents. If you are really pressed for time, acknowledge with

the comment that you are considering the contents and will reply fully at a later date

- In general, your correspondent can assume nothing if you do not reply. Phrases such as: 'If I do not hear from you by . . . you will be deemed to have agreed to my proposal' are meaningless. Sometimes it is wisest to stay silent. An exception is if the contract expressly gives silence a meaning. An example is SBC, clause 3.12.2, where, if you do not dissent from the contractor's confirmation of an oral instruction, the instruction takes effect
- Leave yourself room to manoeuvre in later correspondence
- Try to put yourself in the position of the person who will receive your letter
- Always try to give your correspondent a dignified way out of a difficulty
- If a correspondent is really causing you trouble (some contractors write up to a dozen letters a day about the same project) make a practice of answering all the letters with very short replies – one line if you can manage it
- Pay attention to the arrangement of your letter. Bad news is usually better placed between two sections of good news. This is so that the recipient, in re-reading your letter, is always in the position of having to read some good news with the bad
- Avoid business letter shorthand, e.g. 'ult.', 'inst.', 'even date'
- If writing about a contractual matter, you should use the actual words of the contract to make it clear that you are acting in accordance with the contract or giving some notice or certificate with contractual effect
- Always strive to be honest and direct and confirm exactly what you said orally. It will earn you a good reputation

A final point: communication is best achieved face to face. The next best thing is the telephone. Worst of all is the letter because it can give rise to misunderstandings which cannot be immediately corrected. However, letters are vital as a record of what each party intended at a particular time.

Read the letters in this book critically, bearing these points in mind. They are not carved in granite – merely a guide.

Appendix 2

How to make a good decision

2.01   The problem

This section is intended to express in simple terms how good decisions are made. **Flowchart 7** acts as a summary. You may think this is all nonsense, because you know, or have known, people who can make very quick and correct decisions and they do not go through this process. The truth is that some people can make very rapid and accurate decisions, because they instinctively know the process and they take all the factors into account extremely quickly. Such people are seldom aware that they are going through a process because it is a natural talent. You and I (certainly I) find making good decisions difficult because our minds do not naturally operate in that way. It is, however, a skill which can be acquired.

Unfortunately, this is the kind of thing which sounds rather silly when written down. It sounds as though it should be filed in the same category as 'How to sharpen a pencil'. If you do not need advice about making good decisions, be grateful. For the rest, what follows is intended to sound simple. That is the whole point. If it sounded difficult, it might as well be left unsaid.

Every decision you make is the response to a problem. Most decisions in building, particularly small decisions, are interwoven with other decisions. It is important to focus on them one at a time.

The first thing to clarify is whether the decision you have to make is major or minor, so that you can see how much time needs to be given to it. It is fruitless wasting hours on a decision which has very little implication, even if it is wrong. In order to determine the importance of a decision, you will have to do a little initial analysing. After you have ascertained the importance of the decision you have to make, you can proceed. In the case of major or minor decisions the method is the same; the expenditure of time is different.

Be absolutely clear what really is the problem, or to put it another way, the question you have to ask yourself. It may take some investigation. If you do not properly identify the question, the answer, however ingenious, will be irrelevant. The correct answer to the wrong question is worse than the wrong answer to the correct question. In the latter case at least you have the first part correct (the question) and you can try again until you find the answer. You will never find the answer in the first case, because you have not asked the correct question.

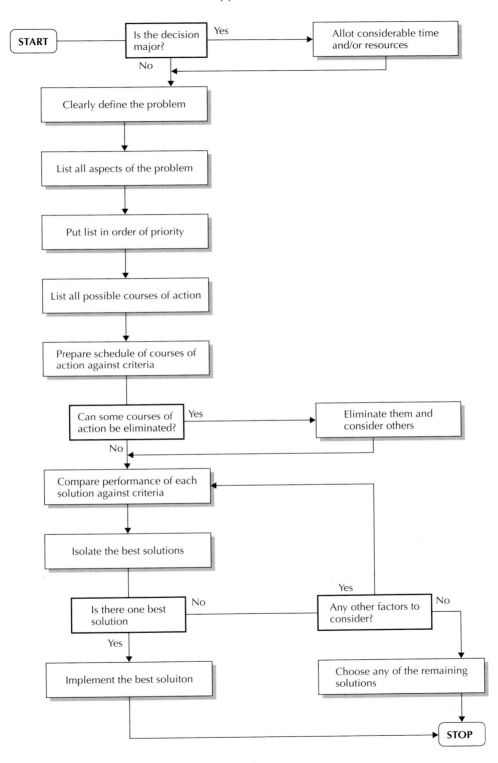

Flowchart 7 Making a decision.

If the problem is major, write it down carefully. The act of writing something down, in itself, concentrates the mind on essentials. Rewrite your definition of the problem until you are absolutely certain that you have put everything down in the least number of words.

2.02   Getting things in order

After the problem has been determined, you must examine all aspects of it. Some people adopt the practice of making a careful written appreciation of every item. Consider all the implications. Put down as many different points as you can, e.g. side-effects, financial or otherwise, opportunities, time scale, special conditions, physical or otherwise. This is best done in note form. Your first list will not have any particular sequence. Jot the points down as they come into your head. The next stage is to do some research to establish any other factors you should take into consideration. Your research will be with colleagues, on site, drawings, bills of quantities, specifications and any other publications which might have a bearing on the problem. By now your list may be pretty extensive.

The next step is to go through your list crossing out duplications and combining items which are closely linked. Prepare a new list by going through your rough draft and identifying the most important consideration and putting it at the top. Carry on this process until all the items are written down in order of importance. You have now assembled all the criteria for your decision and put them in order.

2.03   Alternatives

Take another sheet of paper. This time using the points from sheet 1, note the different possible ways of solving your problem. This is where some ingenuity or lateral thinking is useful to increase the number of possible solutions even if, at first sight, some of them may seem unlikely. At this stage you are probably uncertain whether some of the solutions will work. When you are as certain as you can be that you have covered all possible approaches to the problem, examine each one in turn against the criteria on sheet 1. Some of the solutions will work better than others in different areas. Make a schedule showing the good and bad results against your list of criteria. Some proposed solutions will be eliminated immediately.

2.04   The decision

You now have a sheet showing all the aspects of the problem in order of priority and another sheet listing possible solutions with a rating against each aspect. In some organisations the system has been developed to the point where you actually give numerical values to the ratings and use a complicated method of calculating the best solution. In the context of normal architectural practice such sophisticated techniques are usually unnecessary.

After eliminating the very poor solutions, you will generally have two or three possibles at the most. The decision is then made by comparing the way the solutions satisfy your criteria. In the event that two solutions appear equally satisfactory, for all points of view, you can either re-examine them to see if one is slightly better in some respect which you have hitherto not considered, or you must face the fact that you have two equally good solutions and choose either one.

2.05   When in doubt

There is an old saying: 'When in doubt – do nowt'. Like most old sayings, it contains a grain of truth. It means that if a problem arises which requires your decision and the solution is not immediately obvious, postpone your decision until you have gone through the analytical process described.

At the end of the process, you may find that there is nothing you can do to solve the problem adequately. That is rare. More usually, no solution solves the problem as adequately as you would wish. There are two things you can do. Find another solution or pick the best solution you have.

Of course, you do not have to cover your desk with sheets of paper for every decision you make. In many cases it will be enough to go through the stages in your mind.

The lack of ability to make a decision is really the lack of organised thinking. The mind revolves with a series of ideas, possibilities and fears. The simple exercise outlined in this section should enable you to get your thoughts in order. You may even acquire a reputation for decision-making! At the end of the process you can ask yourself two questions to help your decision:

● What is the worst thing that could happen if my particular decision is wrong?
● What should I *not* do?

Index